Dough Crafts

Dough Crafts

by Isolde Kiskalt

Sterling/Lark

Translation: Net Works, Inc.
Editing: Thom Boswell
Design & Production: Thom Boswell
Typesetting: Elaine Thompson

Kiskalt, Isolde
    [Hobby Salzteig, English]
    Dough crafts / by Isolde Kiskalt.
        p.   cm.
    Translation of: Hobby Salzteig.
    "A Sterling/Lark book—T.p. verso.
    ISBN 0-8069-5842-1
    1. Bread dough craft.   I. Title
TT880.K5713   1991
745.5—dc20

A Sterling/Lark Book

Produced by Altamont Press, Inc.
50 College Street, Asheville, NC 28801

First paperback edition published in 1992 by
    Sterling Publishing Company, Inc.
387 Park Avenue South, New York, N.Y.
    10016

English translation by Networks, Inc. © 1991
    by Altamont Press
First published in Germany under the titles
    Hobby Salzteig © 1983, 1988 and
    Neue zauberhafte salzteig deen ©
    1984, 1987 by Falken-Verlag GmbH,
    Niedemhausen/Ts.

Distributed in Canada by Sterling
    Publishing
% Canadian Manda Group, P.O. Box 920,
    Station U, Toronto, Ontario, Canada
    M8Z 5P9
Distributed in Great Britain and Europe by
    Cassell PLC, Villiers House, 41/47
    Strand, London WC2N 5JE, England
Distributed in Australia by Capricorn Link
    Ltd., P.O. Box 665, Lane Cove, NSW
    2066

Sterling   ISBN 0-8069-5842-1   Trade
             0-8069-5843-X   Paper

Contents

Introduction

When I started modelling beautiful things with saltdough, I never dreamed that this medium would fill me with such enthusiasm.

I've been blessed by the support of my family, who view my creative hobby as an enrichment of their own lives. I especially thank my husband who helped me with all the experiments and refinements of the different techniques.

I am convinced that artistic abilities are dormant in most people, and that they are just waiting to be awakened. I especially realize this during the adult education courses where I teach the manual skills and the history of this old folk art.

One should be aware that by practicing this hobby, an old folk art is being revived which is worth cultivating. In today's technological world, there is a special longing for creative work. Along with the growth of technology, such old customs should be preserved.

Isolde Kiskalt

History of Saltdough

The tradition of giving shape to religious and folklore themes using dough (flour, salt and water) is a very old one. The ancient goddess-worshipping civilization of Crete celebrated its love of Nature through this medium. The classical Egyptians, Greeks and Romans paid homage to their gods by making offerings of dough figures.

During the 19th century in Germany, when the Christmas tree became the focal point of Christmas, the peasants used to make their ornaments from bread dough. To protect them from being eaten by mice or other vermin, they added an especially large amount of salt to the dough. This was the beginning of saltdough.

During World War I, the art of saltdough modelling was almost lost in Europe because there was no salt available to make the dough. About thirty years ago this old folk art was rediscovered, and has since won a considerable following.

MATERIALS

In this section you will be shown the basic techniques of creating saltdough models. Different kinds of dough can be made by varying the flour, salt and water. Methods of shaping and coloring the dough will be explained, as well as drying and baking, painting and varnishing.

The Flour

Standard "all purpose" flour (commonly available in the U.S.) works nicely. Do not use "self-rising" flour. Grinding raw grain results in different flour densities and weight quantities (grinding degree) per 100 g of grain. In order to determine this grinding degree exactly, the flour has to be burnt and the remaining ashes, consisting of minerals, have to be measured.

Wheat flour proves to be somewhat better suited for saltdough than rye flour since the high content of gluten in rye flour causes the air pockets to open wider, making the drying process take relatively longer.

The Salt

The finely granulated table salt (commonly available in the U.S.) is easiest to work with.

You can use less expensive salt as long as it is not too coarse. If necessary, coarse salt can be more finely ground in an electric grinder.

An old coffee grinder is ideal for grinding coarse salt. It should be old since the hard salt crystals quickly dull the blades.

The Workplace and Tools

The temperature of the workroom should not be too warm (no more than 70° F) when working with saltdough, otherwise the dough will become too soft and is difficult to work with. You may have a similar problem if your hands are too warm.

You should have ready:
Flour (wheat and rye), salt, cold water, brush, rolling pin, wooden skewers, toothpicks, modelling tools, small kitchen knife, forks, pocket comb, cookie cutters, round and star-shaped decorating tips, small sieve, garlic press, bottle-caps, pastry cutter and other interesting things to create imaginative patterns on the dough.

Tip: A postage or kitchen scale is ideal for weighing small amounts of dough (up to 20 g), and a ruler will help you stay within the suggested lengths and weights.

The Saltdough Mixtures

Wheat Flour

Depending on what you want to make, the dough requires more flour or more water. If the dough crumbles, add water; if it sticks to your hands, add more flour.

I use the following saltdough mixture:
2 cups wheat flour
1 cup salt
¾ cup water

Once you find the saltdough mixture with which you are most comfortable, you should record that recipe for future reference.

Tip: You can give the dough more elasticity by adding about 1 to 2 teaspoons of wallpaper paste. (Dry paste can be mixed into the dry ingredients, or dissolved paste can be kneaded in. In this case, the amount of water for the dough should be reduced.)

Tip: For children, the dough should be drier, otherwise it becomes too soft in their hands.

Rye Flour

Rye flour adds an attractive brown tone to rustic saltdough models, though they will take longer to dry. Dough made from rye flour alone is quite heavy and therefore difficult to shape. A mixture of wheat and rye flour results in a dough which is easy to work with.

Dough mixture:

3 cups wheat flour	2 cups salt
1 cup rye flour	1½ cups water

Saltdough models containing rye flour should be air-dried for a few days (about a week per ¼" thickness). Then continue drying them very slowly in the oven.

Tip: The weight measures for the models are approximate, since the dough is very heavy. Therefore, it is better to always prepare a bigger amount of rye saltdough.

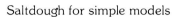

Other Recipes

Dough mixtures can differ greatly. While some people advocate adding wallpaper paste, others add a little bit of vegetable oil or glycerine to the dough. Just as with cooking and baking, everyone has their own special recipe.

For your information:
    1 cup of flour = about 100 g
but: 1 cup of salt = about 200 g

Tip: For dough mixtures using wall-paper paste, take 2 tablespoons of pre-mixed wallpaper paste and mix it with the saltdough.

Saltdough for simple models

    200 g of flour (= 2 cups)
    200 g of salt (= 1 cup)
    125 ccm of water (= ½ cup)

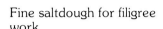

Fine saltdough for filigree work

    200 g of flour (= 2 cups)
    200 g of salt (= 1 cup)
    100 g of corn or potato starch
    150 ccm of water (= ¾ cup)

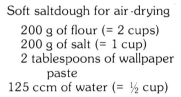

Soft saltdough for air-drying

    200 g of flour (= 2 cups)
    200 g of salt (= 1 cup)
    2 tablespoons of wallpaper paste
    125 ccm of water (= ½ cup)

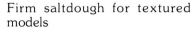

Firm saltdough for textured models

    200 g of flour (= 2 cups)
    400 g of salt (= 2 cups)
    125 ccm of water (= ½ cup)

Firm saltdough for tiles and plates

    200 g of flour (= 2 cups)
    400 g of salt (= 2 cups)
    2 tablespoons of wallpaper paste
    125 ccm of water (= ½ cup)

Important: The dough should be covered whenever you are not using it. It dries out very quickly when it is left uncovered.

Small medallions can be shaped in many ways. Based on your own pref-erence, they can be painted, left natural, or formed with colored dough.

These models show how delicately saltdough can be modelled. They are shown at almost their original size.

Kneading

Before the saltdough is workable, it has to be kneaded thoroughly until it is smooth, otherwise it may crack or crumble.

Making a large amount of dough, or making saltdough fairly often, can be tiresome work which may possibly strain your wrists and arms. Using an electric handmixer or a food processor with a kneading attachment makes the mechanical process of making saltdough much easier. Processing with a machine is much faster and more thorough than doing it by hand.

Tip: When using regular food processors, work only small amounts of dough or the machine may overheat. (Read the instruction manual for your appliance.)

Processing

The best flour to use in the U.S. is "all-purpose" flour. In Europe there are many types of flour on the market which can differ very much—even from region to region. You cannot deduce the percentage of starch in the flour from the name "Type 405." Type 405 indicates the grinding degree and means that 405 mg of minerals are left in the ashes after the burning test.

With a basic dough mixture of

200 g of flour (= 2 cups)
200 g of salt (= 1 cup)
125 ccm of water (= ½ cup)

the amount of water should not exceed the given amount by much. If you need to double the amount of water for the above recipe, the kind of flour you're using is not suitable for making salt-dough. You can improve the workable quality of your flour by adding corn starch, potato starch, or any other food starch.

Tip: For processing saltdough you should use a brand of flour that needs only a small amount of water for a good dough mixture. That means that the flour should have a high starch content.

Tip: Flour that needs a lot of water to make the dough workable makes the dough rise a lot while drying in the oven, causing cracking due to strain.

Storing

It is ideal to prepare only as much dough as you can work at one time, since fresh dough is best for modelling. However, leftover dough can be stored in airtight plastic containers or wrapped tightly in plastic wrap or aluminum foil.

Kept in a cool place (*not* in the refrigerator, however) the dough will remain fresh for a few days and can, if necessary, again be mixed with flour and salt before you resume working with it.

Two useful aids for kneading are the food processor and a handheld electric mixer.

The cross section of this object shows clearly that the model has been dried too quickly and at too high a temperature. The dough has risen and air bubbles have formed, which has produced cracks.

Assembling with Dough Paste

When you are using fresh dough, it is usually sufficient to moisten the parts that you wish to connect at the seams and to press them together.

However, some objects are the result of several working steps, and you are modelling over already dried parts. If you were to moisten these parts only with water in order to connect them, these added parts would separate again after the drying process.

Therefore, to connect previously dried parts with moist parts you need a special gluing material. Instead of water, use fresh saltdough paste. In other words, take a small amount of dough and turn it into a paste by adding water (a small amount) and stirring it with a modelling tool. Use this as your gluing compound.

Repairing Dried Models

You can also make paste from dried saltdough scraps by grinding saltdough crumbs in a mortar (or similar container) into a powder, and mixing this powder with some water into a paste.

This method can be easily applied to parts which have broken off a dried object and cannot be used again. With this special paste, the missing parts can either be replaced or reconnected.

Tip: If you use paste on browned or painted parts, or if you want to repair them, you should try to match the original color with paint after drying.

Dried saltdough crumbs are ground into a fine powder in a mortar.

The sheep's defective legs are replaced with newly modelled ones, and connected at the break with saltdough paste.

Modelling on Surfaces

It is easier to shape dough directly on a cookie sheet. In this way, the back of the model becomes smooth, and you avoid the risk of damage while transferring the model to the cookie sheet. Wet the cookie sheet with a moist brush before you begin modelling. This prevents air bubbles between cookie sheet and dough.

If you are modelling on aluminum foil and you put the model on the foil in the oven, the underside needs a substantially longer time for drying. Aluminum foil is ideal for covering parts which are becoming too dark during the browning process, such as leaves on a wreath.

Drying and Baking

Drying is the most important step because it is very disappointing to see your beautiful work crack due to baking too quickly or incorrectly. General rules for baking include placing the cookie sheet on the top rack until the surface of the dough turns white. After that, it cannot lose its shape. Then move the cookie sheet to the middle rack. More top heat would only be needed for browning. If the model begins to warp—if it rises up from the cookie sheet—the temperature is too high. If you don't reduce the temperature, the underside of the model will crack.

Air-Drying

This takes a long time but saves electricity or gas. The underside of the model does not stay flat but shows a curvature. The soft dough pulls inward because the water evaporates during the drying process. It takes about one day of air-drying per 1/16″ of thickness. During the summer you can use the sun for drying. Simply put the models in the sunlight.

This method is especially suited for thick models to save energy, but it can take several weeks, depending on the thickness of the model. Air-dried objects can still be browned weeks later.

If you air-dry wreaths and then wish to finish the drying in the oven, you should start with a low temperature. The inside pressure could otherwise get too high, and the models might burst open.

Tip: You will find holes on the underside of air-dried (not yet browned) models. They are caused by the loss of moisture. These holes can be closed again with fresh dough or with thick paste after first moistening the area.

Tip: For models that are to be air-dried only, mix wallpaper paste into the dough for increased firmness. The starch content in the flour starts reacting only at a temperature of about 160° F, and then only in conjunction with water.

Important: *Thin models* should either be *air-dried only* or *oven-dried only*. The combined drying (air and oven) creates strain in flat models which can later cause cracks.

Drying in the Gas Oven

A gas oven needs only half the baking time of the electric oven. Since natural gas has a high degree of moisture, saltdough models dry very slowly at the surface. As a result, the model's inner moisture can evaporate very well. Since the thermostat setting for the gas oven may be higher than that of an electric oven, you can regulate it by slightly opening the oven door.

The drying process in the gas oven for a tree, for example:

first hour: half-open oven door at lowest temperature
second hour: quarter-open oven door at lowest temperature
third hour: closed oven door at lowest temperature

For the browning process you should turn the temperature to 400° F and then carefully watch the browning.

Tip: The immediate closing of the oven door will result in unattractive air bubbles in the saltdough models.

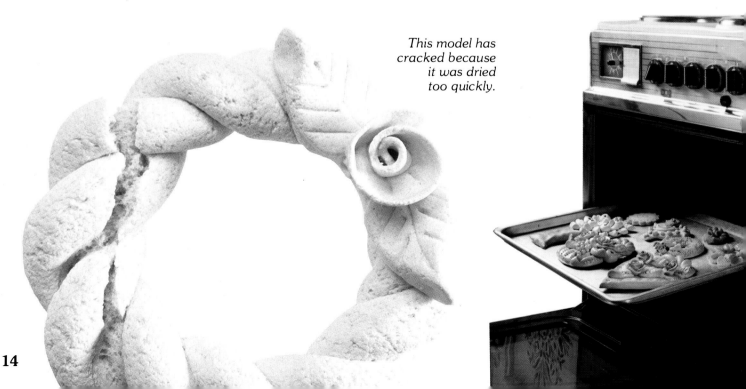

This model has cracked because it was dried too quickly.

Drying in the Electric Oven With or Without Upper and Lower Heat

Both types of ovens are well suited for the drying and baking of saltdough models. The only differences are in the use of light or dark cookie sheets, since they reach different temperatures at the same temperature setting of the oven.

Light cookie sheet:
Per ¼″ thickness of the model you can allow one hour at about 170° F. Thus, for a thickness of 1½″, you will need about 6 hours at 170° F.

After this, adjust the temperature to 200° F, then 250° F, then 300° F. These hotter stages of baking are *not* influenced by the thickness of a model but are used for all models.

To measure the thickness of a model, use a wooden skewer and a ruler.

For each model:
½ hour at 200° F
½ hour at 250° F
1 hour at 300° F

After these baking times, the salt-dough models should be thoroughly dry. Following the baking, you can still brown them at 400° F.

Tip: The browning process should definitely be watched closely so that you get the degree of browning you want.

Important: When you are using *dark baking sheets*, you must reduce the above mentioned temperatures by 70° F.

Drying in the Convection Oven

Because of the circulation of heat, the surface dries much more quickly in a convection oven than it does with any other drying method. This can be quite handy in some circumstances, such as when you add to a thicker model whose contours are already firm.

For the drying process in general, the drying is stopped on the surface as soon as a crust forms. From this moment, the final drying of the model proceeds very slowly.

Conclusion:
The drying process in the convection oven can take longer than in the electric oven (with or without upper and lower heat).

Electricity consumption:
Even though the temperature is lower than in the common electric oven, you still have to count on a longer baking time. A substantial saving of electricity can only be obtained by drying several cookie sheets at the same time in the oven.

Tip: A microwave oven is not suited for the drying of saltdough. During tests with different appliances, the dough always rose rapidly and then collapsed.

The drying times for colored ¼″ thick saltdough models:

1 hour at 150° F.
½ hour at 200° F.
½ hour at 250° F.
1 hour at 270° F.

Depending on the thickness of the saltdough model, the first hour at 150° F may have to be prolonged.

Important: Models made with colored dough (except cocoa) should not be baked at more than 250° F, otherwise the colors change.

Tip: As a result of this very slow drying and/or baking process, all pieces come out of the oven completely hard and dried inside, and without cracking.

Testing for Dryness

How do you know whether the pieces are completely dry?

Tap your index finger on the surface. If it sounds dull, the model is still moist inside and should stay in the oven. If it sounds like hardened clay, the model is dry.

If a modelled part has already come off the cookie sheet, you can pick it up with a pot-holder and tap it on the back to check the drying.

Browning the Dough

As soon as you are sure that the pieces are dry, turn the oven temperature to 400° F. To get the desired degree of browning, it is advisable to stay close by and watch. The brown tone deepens even more with the application of varnish. If some parts of the model begin to turn very dark during the browning process, they should be covered with aluminum foil.

Tip: If you are not sure if the pieces will be the desired shade of brown when varnished, you can carefully go over some of the lighter and darker areas with a moist brush. This will show you what the brown will look like after the application of varnish.

Three degrees of browning

Coloring the Dough

Food coloring can be added one drop at a time to the finished saltdough mixture made with wheat flour. If you want to use only one color, you can add food coloring directly to the flour-salt-water mixture. Otherwise separate the dough mixture into as many parts as you want colors.

Tip: First shape the part of dough that is to be colored into a ball and press a dent into the middle. Drop the desired amount of food coloring in the depression and fold the dough carefully over. Knead until the dough ball is evenly colored.

Per 100 g of dough:

2 drops blue

5 drops red

2 drops yellow

2 drops green

Purple: 3 drops red and 1 drop blue

Brown: add 1 teaspoon unsweetened cocoa (and water if necessary), or instant coffee dissolved in a little water.

Painting

It is a matter of taste which shades of colors you choose to paint the models. On the pictured "color wreaths," we demonstrate how you can change a basic color of watercolors to lighter or darker shades.

The colors are mixed as follows:

Basic color plus white = pastel white
Basic color alone
Basic color plus the next darker
    shade of the same color
Basic color plus burnt umber
    (brown) = muted shade of color

Tip: You should first apply a white primer on saltdough models that you wish to paint. Do not paint until the primer is dry.

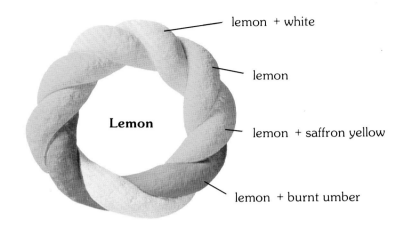

lemon + white
lemon
lemon + saffron yellow
lemon + burnt umber
Lemon

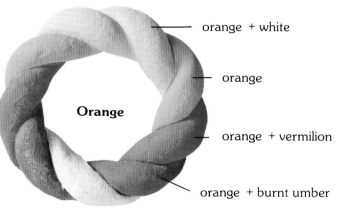

orange + white
orange
orange + vermilion
orange + burnt umber
Orange

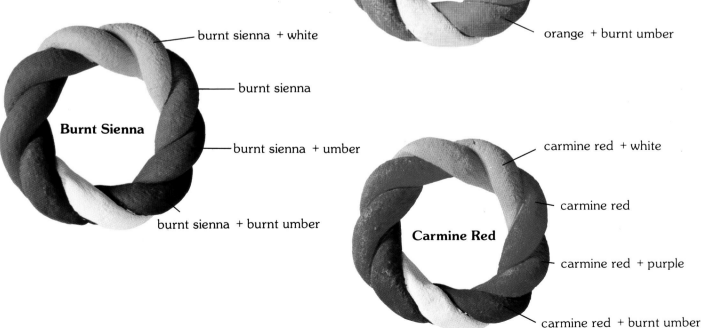

burnt sienna + white
burnt sienna
burnt sienna + umber
burnt sienna + burnt umber
Burnt Sienna

carmine red + white
carmine red
carmine red + purple
carmine red + burnt umber
Carmine Red

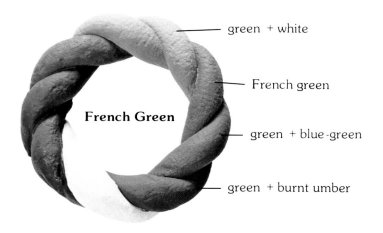

green + white

French green

French Green

green + blue-green

green + burnt umber

In order to get brilliant colors and a smooth surface, you should first apply a primer on the pieces. You can use either Chinese White or a white wall primer. Watercolors are ideally suited for the actual coloring.

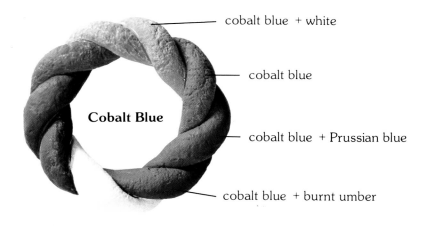

cobalt blue + white

cobalt blue

Cobalt Blue

cobalt blue + Prussian blue

cobalt blue + burnt umber

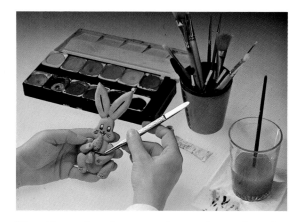

Tip: If cracks show on the surface after the drying of the paint, either the paint has been applied too thickly or the type of paint used has had a chemical reaction with the saltdough. In this case try a different brand of paint.

purple + white

purple

Purple

purple + Prussian blue

purple + burnt umber

Coloring by Baking and Glazing

Even without using color, you can alter the surface of your saltdough models.

The Alkaline Effect:
Brush the models during the last hour in the 300° F oven with a mixture of corn (and/or beet) syrups and water.

Even Coloring in Beige-Brown with a "Salt Glaze":
Brush the parts several times with saltwater during the last hour in a 300° F oven. If a deeper brown is desired, turn the temperature up to 400° F and then apply the salt glaze.

Tip: The salt glaze is created by salt crystals dissolving on the surface. Therefore, the glazed parts will need very little varnish.

White:
The surface stays white with air-drying or with drying in the oven at a temperature not higher than 250° F.

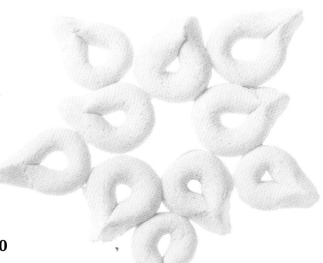

Looking Like Yeast Pastry:
First put a salt glaze on the models during the last hour in the 300° F oven. Then brush the models, either with a mixture of milk and water, or egg yolk and water. Depending on how deep a brown tone is desired, turn the temperature as high as 400° F.

Varnishing

There are different kinds of clear varnish: thinner ones and thicker ones. Thin varnish, in cans or sprays, gives the saltdough model little protection. It soaks into the dough and the models therefore have to be coated several times, which still will not last. It is, however, possible to use varnish with a thin consistency if the brown tones are supposed to be brought out more strongly without giving the model the gloss of varnish.

By contrast, two coats of varnish with a thick consistency offers excellent protection against time and humidity. This does require that the models be varnished on all sides. If you don't like high gloss, you can use matte finish varnish instead. After many years, you may need to apply another coat.

I recommend clear varnish like polyurethane, particularly the type used for boats or wooden floors. It comes in matte, semi-gloss, and high-gloss finishes.

Important: Saltdough models that have been varnished without having dried out completely may lose their appeal after a while because the varnish will flake and peel off.

FORMING TECHNIQUES

Cutting Dough with Cookie Cutters

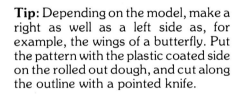

Tip: Depending on the model, make a right as well as a left side as, for example, the wings of a butterfly. Put the pattern with the plastic coated side on the rolled out dough, and cut along the outline with a pointed knife.

With a rolling pin, roll the dough to a thickness of about ¼", either on your working area or right on the

cookie sheet. Then press cookie cutters of your choice, spaced closely together, into the dough.

Making Patterns

Working with patterns does not mean that you are unable to be creative. For a beginner, a predesigned pattern can be a big help in getting started, while original designs are a great help for the more advanced in creating a complicated model.

If you give your saltdough models as gifts, you should consider collecting the patterns and keeping them in a plastic bag. Copying a certain model later is rather tedious with a pattern. Draw the desired outline on the noncoated side of laminated cardboard (such as the cardboard commonly inserted into a commercially pressed shirt) and cut it out.

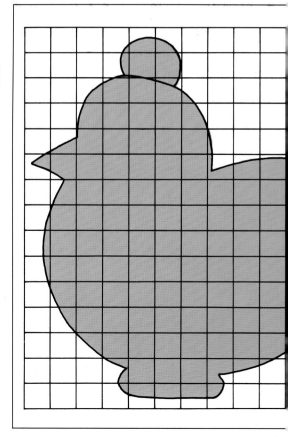

Cutting Dough Using a Pattern

Roll dough to a ¼″ thickness on your working surface or cookie sheet. Then place a traced or handmade pattern on the dough and cut with a sharp knife along the sides of the pattern. Remove the pattern carefully. Moisten the edges with water, then smooth them with a modelling tool.

You can assemble dough parts by wetting them with a moist brush. This lets the gluten content in the flour act like glue. If you want to place pieces on top of each other, you should moisten the underside of the upper piece with water so that no water stains show on the top side of the model. If you want to be completely sure the piece is evenly wet, moisten the whole object with water before putting it in the oven.

Important: For the patterns, use laminated cardboard because it is water-resistant. Pieces of dough left on the laminated surface can be removed with a dough scraper. Untreated cardboard sticks to the dough.

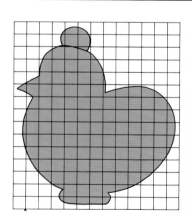

Enlarging and Reducing
First draw a grid pattern across the desired motif. If you want to reduce the motif, draw a corresponding smaller grid. Transfer the intersecting points of the motif onto the smaller grid and trace the contours. Reverse the steps for enlarging a motif.

The Twisted Wreath

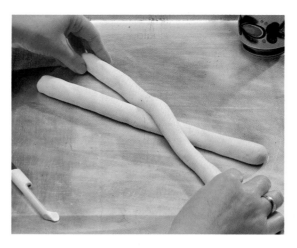

To make ropes for twisting or braiding, first shape the dough into a thick oblong roll. Place hands flat, with closed fingers, at the center. Then roll the dough back and forth while spreading your fingers.

The twisted wreath is made with two equally long ropes of dough. Cross the two ropes in the middle and twist them away from the center. Start in the middle so that you end up with equally thick ropes of dough when you close the wreath.

Closing the twisted wreath

Cut all four ends straight, moisten them and press together.

Or, connect the ends by tapering the ends of the ropes. Though this method is more complicated, it guarantees better durability.

For this method, cut the end of one rope diagonally downward and the corresponding one diagonally upward. Moisten and press together.

Repeat the procedure with the second rope. This is the best way to close the wreath.

TIP: These two methods for joining wreaths can also be used for the braided wreath (page 26).

Isolde Kiskalt

The Braided Wreath

The braiding technique uses three equally long and equally thick ropes of dough. For a short braid, start at one end and work toward the other. For long braids, start in the middle to prevent the ropes from stretching while you are working. Otherwise they would get thinner at the ends and when you tried to close the braid into a wreath, you would have to connect a thick end with a thin one.

If you want a braided wreath with a specific diameter, multiply the diameter by three to determine how long the ropes should be.

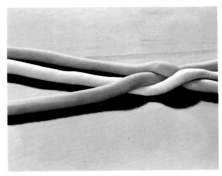

The dough ropes are placed over each other on the right side.

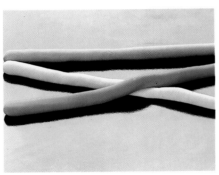

We marked the three dough ropes with different colors for clarity.

The dough ropes are placed under each other on the left side.

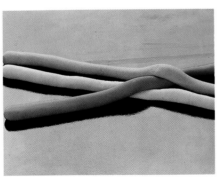

When making longer braids, it is also advisable to start working from the center.

Close the wreath using the same technique used for the twisted wreath, blending to eliminate seams.

Tip: If you start braiding from the center, you have to remember to put the dough ropes over each other on one side, whereas you put them under each other when you are working in the opposite direction.

Tip: Adding more flour and perhaps some wallpaper paste to the dough will make it more supple and less likely to tear: 3 cups flour, 1 cup salt, about 3 tablespoons wallpaper paste and about 1 cup of water.

Working with Tools

By using differently shaped objects and tools, you can create interesting effects with your saltdough models. You can press a pattern into the dough with a toothpick, for example, or a wooden skewer. It is also possible to create a rough surface on the dough using these tools.

Structuring with Decorating Tips
Decorating tips pressed into the dough result in attractive round or star-shaped patterns.

Effects with a Strainer
Pressing the dough through a strainer creates tiny dough "noodles." For this technique, the dough has to be prepared with very fine salt.
(See page 11.)

Tip: The dough should be dry and smooth before pressing it through the strainer.

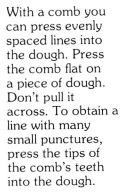

With a comb you can press evenly spaced lines into the dough. Press the comb flat on a piece of dough. Don't pull it across. To obtain a line with many small punctures, press the tips of the comb's teeth into the dough.

Small strands of dough made with a garlic press

Using a garlic press instead of a sieve will give you spaghetti-like strings of dough which can be used as hair, fur or other decorations.

Making Coarse and Delicate Textures

You can create different surface textures with the help of various household utensils.

Fine Texture

Roughen the surface evenly with a bamboo skewer.

Rough Texture

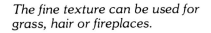

Pull off uneven sized bits from a larger piece of dough.

The fine texture can be used for grass, hair or fireplaces.

The rough texture gives a natural look to a treetop. It is ideal for grassy areas as well.

Pressing heavy lace or lace curtains into the dough will result in this "lacy design."

The hair and coat trim of this figure use medium and rough textures.

The mask's hair, the dog's coat, and the sheep's wool have all been textured with a garlic press.

Fine dough threads which you get with a strainer can be used for fur, hair and similar things.

The garlic-pressed dough strands are ideal fur or hair for larger models.

Grooving the dough with a knife gives it a nice wood grain effect.

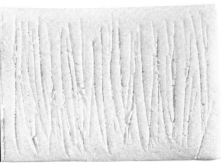

Pressing Objects into Dough

Pressing objects (i.e. buttons, grasses) into the dough will create imprints. For example: you can press buttons which have an interesting shape or pattern into the dough. To make it easier to remove the buttons from the dough you should make a button "stamp": Glue a button on the end of a wooden peg. If the underside of the button is not flat, drill a hole or an indentation into the peg. For buttons with holes, use enough glue to fill the holes.

Rollers which are already engraved with a decorative pattern can also be used to texture the dough's surface.

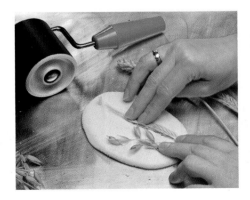

First press grasses, grain stalks, or other plants lightly into the dough with your fingers.

Then roll over it carefully and evenly with a rolling pin, starting at the stems and rolling upward.

Remove the grasses and any remnants afterwards using pointed tweezers or by hand.

Tip: The dough should be dry and smooth to get clearly visible imprints.

Pressing Dough into Molds

Pressing the dough into carved-out objects (butter molds, etc.) creates a raised pattern on the dough when removed from the mold. These are positive contours.

When working with butter molds, the dough should be made with very fine salt in order to get clearly defined contours. Lightly flour the mold with a brush and then press the dough in, starting at one side. Be very careful when you remove the dough from the mold!

You can also use an easier technique and get the same result. Roll the dough to a thickness of about ½". Press the floured mold firmly into the dough, and then lift it carefully off. Next cut the rough edges of the dough completely straight using a sharp knife. Afterwards clean the mold with water and a soft brush. Let it dry at room temperature, never on a radiator!

You can use all kinds of molds as long as the pattern is not too deep.

Tip: You can create your own positive and negative molds with Fimo modelling material (available at most hobby/craft stores). After baking, the Fimo molds can be used for a long time.

Basket Textures

By using different tools you can create various basket designs.

You get a fine texture with pointed tweezers.

Press very fine lines into the dough with one of the modelling tools.

This design is the result of two forks pressed together.

Press the dough together with a marzipan tool.

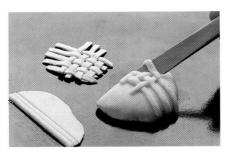

"Weave" a basket pattern with strips of dough.

Designs of Crete

An especially beautiful way of making ornamental bread comes from the isle of Crete, where wedding wreaths and other symbolic models are crafted. On Crete, modelling with bread dough is an ancient tradition.

One common component of wreaths is leaves. To make leaves of the same size, cut a roll of dough into slices of even thickness. Knead and roll each slice between your hands into a ball. Then put these dough balls on the working surface and flatten them. Pinch dough into a pointed tip with thumb and index finger. Now you can press the veins into the leaf using a modelling tool. Other interesting designs can be produced with the help of combs and marzipan tools.

Press the comb with the flat side on a slice of dough. You can arrange the pieces into different shapes.

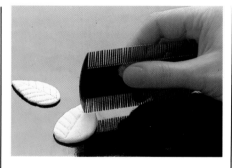

Prick holes into the leaves using the teeth of the comb. You achieve double rows by using a marzipan tool.

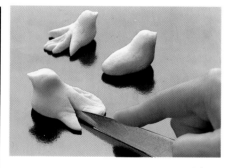

You can structure the wings with a comb. You can do the same to the tail or you can make incisions with a knife.

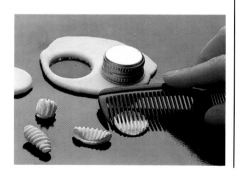

Making Delicate Flowers

You can also do filigree and other very delicate work with saltdough. In order to do so you have to prepare a fine saltdough (see recipe, page 11).

The size of the flowers being modelled depends on your dexterity and is, in general, a matter of practice. If you want to shape several of the same kind of flowers, it is better to cut slices of even thickness from one roll of dough for the petals. Another possibility is to roll the dough flat and cut out the petals with a small round cookie cutter.

For a nice effect with roses, press the petals with your fingers until they are very thin at their outer edges. Loosen them very carefully, starting with the thicker side, using a knife before forming them into a rose.

Roses look quite decorative when they are made with a thin ribbon of dough. The length of the ribbon depends on the size of the objects you want to decorate. Experiment first by rolling the dough into a ribbon about 2½″ long and ½″ wide. Place the ribbon on the palm of your hand extending to your fingertips. Roll it up, starting at your fingertips. Once the center has been formed you can fold the rest of the ribbon loosely around it (the last part can even be pleated). With a toothpick pushed through the center of the rose you can attach the flower to the desired object.

Leaves and Blossoms

Press the dough flat to form delicate leaves. Blossoms can be made by pressing notches into dough balls with a modelling tool.

Pointed Petals

Cut out the blossom with a small cookie cutter, make an incision between each petal and roll the petal tips around a bamboo skewer.

Ball-Shaped Flowers

Connect little dough balls and, with a bamboo skewer, either prick in little holes or little notches.

Joining Petals

Small flower petals can be assembled in many different ways; you can press them flat or leave them thicker at the tips.

Anemones

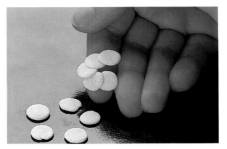

Anemones are created by placing five slices over each other. The center can be a dough ball or a juniper berry.

Roses

The thinner you press the dough edges, the more delicate will be the roses. You can shape them from a dough ribbon or from single petals.

37

Floral Ideas

Making Spines

You can achieve a beautiful effect by cutting spines out of the dough for a hedgehog, or by giving feathers to an owl or other birds.

Cut the dough carefully at an angle where you want texture using sharp scissors (maybe even a pair of curved scissors). Depending on the dough's density, the cut feathers will stick out. But since they might easily break off, it is advisable to smooth the feathers or spines very carefully with a dry brush or to gently push the tips down. This also gives it a more natural look.

The spines are indented with sharp scissors. The size of the scissors determines the size of the spines.

The spines can be carefully pressed back with a dry brush.

Tip: To shorten the baking time for these hedgehogs, they have been modelled over little support cones which can be removed after cooling.

Making Support Cones

For creating taller models it is best to make little support cones out of plastic coated cardboard.

You can calculate the desired size as follows:

    Height x 2 = diameter of the desired circle
    Example: desired height = 2 inches, so 2 x 2 = 4 inches in diameter

In this case you should cut out a circle with a 4-inch diameter.

Make a cut to the center of the circle and let the cardboard overlap until you have the desired circumference (base). Secure the cone on the inside as well as the outside with tape.

Depending on the model you can make a high, pointed, flat or wide cone.

Pull the cardboard across the blade of a knife or scissors to round it more easily.

The Aluminum Foil Technique

Aluminum foil is extremely well suited for "upholstering" thick models. Crumple the foil up and press it into the appropriate shape. The saltdough coat should be about ¼″ thick when shaped around the aluminum center. Cover the aluminum foil completely with saltdough until it is no longer visible.

The saltdough has been rolled flat.

A finished hedgehog has been cut open: aluminum foil and coat of saltdough are clearly recognizable.

The aluminum ball is covered and closed up with saltdough.

Hollow Models

Hollowing Out

Whenever you make a thick model and you wish to shorten the drying process you can hollow out the models. Put them on aluminum foil so that they don't stick to the cookie sheet. After about two hours of baking time at 120° F to 160° F (electric oven) take the parts out of the oven. Hold them carefully in your hand (with a pot-holder) and pull the foil off. Then hollow them out.

The outer coat or outer layer should already be dried to a thickness of about 1/16″ before you start so that it won't get deformed during the process of hollowing it out. You can carefully take out a part of the inner, moist dough with the use of a melon cutter. You should leave a wall of about ¼″ thickness.

After the model has dried out and cooled off completely, the cracks that occurred inside can be closed with a thick glue.

Carefully pull off the aluminum foil from the moist base.

With a melon cutter scrape the dough out of the interior.

Important: You have to work very carefully when using this technique or you might crush the model.

Tip: It is better to use support cones for the thicker models.

Tip: The energy savings are quite high with hollow models—up to half the drying time! This can be quite important for electric oven users.

Making Vases

Take a small vase and cover it completely and evenly on the outside with saltdough, except the bottom. Cut the saltdough covering into two halves; this will enable you to take the dough off the vase after the baking process.

During the drying process, the dough will contract without being stressed and without cracking.

As soon as both halves of the vase are thoroughly dry and cool, they can be carefully taken off the mold.

The two halves are put together and connected with saltdough paste and moist saltdough and then dried again.

Making Bowls

By using auxiliary molds made out of ceramic, oven-proof or similar materials, you can make corresponding models from saltdough. You can coat them partially on the inside as well as on the outside. If you cover them on the outside you can put a pattern into the outer wall of the saltdough with tweezers, for example.

If you coat the mold on the inside you can distribute the dough very carefully from the center of the bottom up to the rim to avoid air bubbles. The saltdough will come off the mold by itself as soon as it is completely dry.

Different molds may be coated with dough on the inside or on the outside. Depending on the model, *you may create a basketweave with the help of tweezers.*

Important: You should be careful that the saltdough can be slipped off the mold. That is not possible, for example, if the container narrows at the upper *and* the lower part. The saltdough coat should only be removed from the mold after having *completely* dried.

Tip: The dough mixture should consist of firm saltdough to which wallpaper paste has been added (see recipe, page 11).

Tip: The auxiliary mold may be coated with a little bit of oil.

Tip: There will be almost no tension in the dough when coating the inside of a mold since the dough can contract according to its degree of drying. That is not possible to such an extent when coating the outside of a mold.

As soon as the coat of the vase has cooled, put it on freshly rolled out dough and cut out the bottom piece.

Connect the bottom and the top with paste, and dry it again.

Making Reliefs and Plaques

High reliefs can be created using different construction methods.

1. The saltdough is modelled without a background (base), and then is later glued on a different material. This material can be wood, cork, a bulletin board or cloth.

2. The saltdough picture is modelled on a saltdough base. The base has been made from saltdough with wallpaper paste added. The picture itself can be worked from regular, fine, or supple saltdough (see recipes, page 11).

3. The saltdough picture is being modelled on an already baked saltdough tile. With this assembly you should use saltdough "paste" for better adhesion (see "Connecting Model Parts," page 13). For a special effect you can dye or color the tile brown and leave the addition in the natural saltdough look.

The finished saltdough model is glued on a cork base.

You continue modelling on a moist saltdough base.

Important: To avoid waterstains on the tile or saltdough base, the added parts should always be moistened on the underside. The saltdough base should not be exposed to a temperature shock or it might break in half.

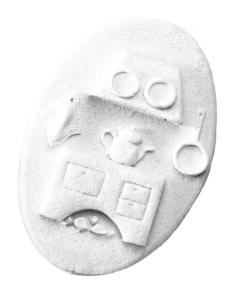

The saltdough base has been baked and browned first. After the cooling you can begin the picture.

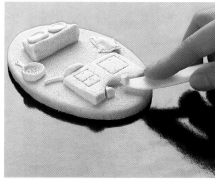

44

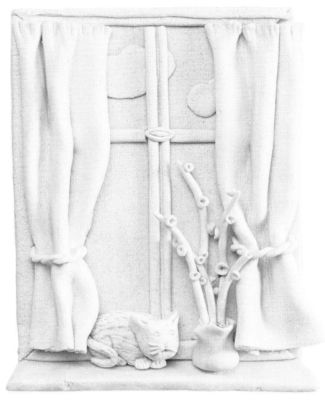

Making Picture Frames

Select the shape you want for a plate—round, oval or angular—and form a saltdough frame around it. Frames for round or oval plates are the easiest. You roll a rope of dough, place it around the moistened base and close it to form a frame. Both ends should be carefully connected so that the seam is not visible.

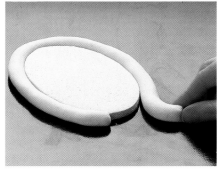

A rope of dough is placed around a moistened base.

There is also another way of framing. Roll a rope of dough to twice the thickness of the desired frame. Press half the rope flat with a round object and you will get a picture frame with a ledge. Moisten the edges of the plate and carefully add the ledges. Press the ledge firmly against the plate with a modelling tool. The thick part will bulge over the plate while the thin part sticks to the edge of the plate.

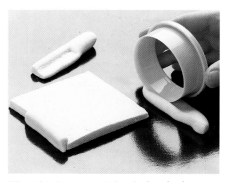

The thick part of the ledge bulges over the base plate, the thin one sticks to its edge.

Tip: You can glue picture hangers to the back of a varnished model. Picture hangers are sold in different sizes. Choose the size appropriate to the model's weight. The load-bearing strength is normally indicated on the package.

For angular frames, you may choose from three procedures:

1. Exactly as you did with the round or oval frame, put the ledge around the dough plate, lightly define the corners and close the ledge to form a frame.

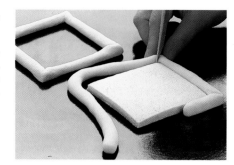

2. Cut the ledge parts straight and connect them with the dough plate.

3. Make a bevelled edge; cut the ends of the ledge at an angle.

Marbleizing

Kneading together dough ropes which have been dyed in various colors gives you a marbleizing effect. The mixed dough must be kneaded until the desired veining has been achieved.

Tip: Don't knead the dough too long, or you might lose the effect completely.

Special Effects:

Drip different food colors on the flattened dough and roll it up. Then cut off thin or thicker slices. By pressing or pulling with your fingers you can create lovely color patterns.

A few drops of food coloring are added to rolled out dough.

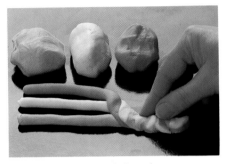

Differently colored dough parts are kneaded together.

The dough is rolled up and sliced. Pulling and pressing it will create color patterns.

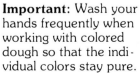

Important: Wash your hands frequently when working with colored dough so that the individual colors stay pure.

Heart-Shaped Bowl

For shaping, use an existing mold which simultaneously serves as support. After the drying is complete, the saltdough will be separated from the mold.

Tip: Use firm dough with wallpaper paste (see recipe, page 11) for this bowl.

Beaded Necklace

Little balls are rolled from marbleized dough and pierced on two sides with a toothpick covered with flour.

First, the beads are air-dried on the toothpicks until they keep their shape (about 2 hours). Then the toothpicks are removed and the beads are dried in the oven.

The beads are put back on toothpicks for the varnishing process.

Tip: The toothpicks may be stuck into a piece of floral foam or something similar to keep them upright.

Important: The oven temperature should not exceed 250° F for colored dough or the colors will change.

The beads are pierced on two sides with a toothpick covered with flour.

To dry, the beads are stuck on toothpicks which are placed in floral foam.

Assembling a Figure

Shape a thick, long roll of dough for the body and legs. Make a cut halfway through the dough for the legs.

The legs may be rounded. If they are too thick you can cut off some dough. Shape the head from a thicker ball of dough and add it to the body.

Now you can start clothing the doll (see facing page). The steps for adding the clothing must be done in sequence.

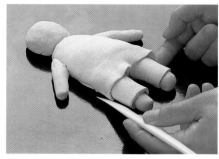

Modelling Hair

Hair can be created in different ways. Depending on the size of the head and the desired hairstyle, you can use roughened parts of dough for a curly hairstyle; you can shape fine strands of hair with a strainer, rougher ones with a garlic press, or you can cut the hairstyle from a pattern. Roll out the dough thinly, cut out the area of the hair, and mark the part. Then cut fine strands of hair almost up to the part, but make sure the strands are separated at the tips. This way they can be arranged nicely after you place them on the head.

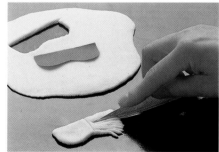

Attach the straight cut edge to the back of the head. Bangs may be added to the front indentation.

You can shape dolls in different proportions:

The drawing on the left shows a proportion where the head size fits seven times into the size of the body. These proportions are well suited for "adult" figures such as the vagabond.

The drawing on the right gives proportions where the head fits three times into the body. You can use these proportions for smaller saltdough dolls and children.

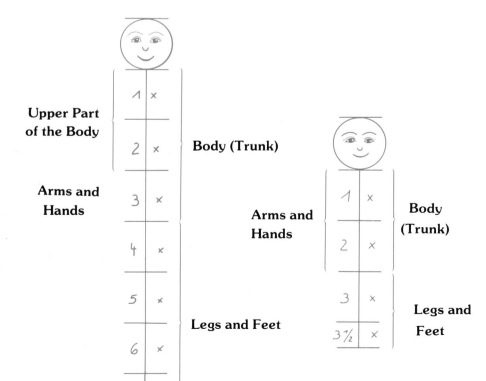

Upper Part of the Body

Arms and Hands

Body (Trunk)

Legs and Feet

Arms and Hands

Body (Trunk)

Legs and Feet

Making Patterns

Knowing how to design the clothing adds a very personal touch to your dolls.

Depending on the assembly, you can start with the underwear and continue "dressing" the doll. Once you have finished modelling the body, head, arms, and legs, and you want to start the clothing, you can design each pattern on wax paper as shown in the photos.

Put an appropriate piece of wax paper over the model and cut it to size with small scissors.

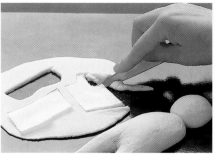

Then place the wax paper on thinly rolled dough and cut it out. With this method you are able to dress the entire doll family—each of them differently. Thus, in addition, you become a "saltdough tailor."

The vagabond has many beautiful details.

This little sandman seems to be especially friendly because of the choice of colors.

Assembling Sculptures

Forming sculptures from saltdough is a tedious job, but the result is very attractive. Saltdough is a heavy dough which cannot keep its shape after a certain height (about 2¼″) because of its own weight. Therefore you have to compensate for this disadvantage by using two different working methods.

1. See instructions in "Making Support Cones," page 41.

2. You start modelling a doll usually beginning with the front. You have to take into account that the back part has to be added on later. The front part of the doll can be dried in the usual way. As soon as it is completely dry and cool, the missing back part of the doll can be modelled on.

Important: Place the finished half of the model on a thick soft towel before you continue with the modelling so that nothing will be damaged and no parts break off.

Before you add the back, you have to file down the edges of the model and attach the missing parts in a rough structure.

Tip: Follow the instructions step by step! Hair, for example, can only be attached after the collar has been modelled.

The clothing is modelled in folds which curve away from the body.

The edges are smoothed with a file.

The contours of the figure have to be finished before the clothing can be added.

The connecting lines are smoothed over to avoid visible seams.

Tip: Balance will be achieved with the shoes once the gnome is fully dried.

This little buddha shows how well saltdough can be used to model faces.

Night Watchman

Working with Plants

Are they really just weeds? If you look closely at the side of the road or the edge of woods or in fields, you will easily find decorative touches for salt-dough models. Many common weeds, such as baby's breath, statice, and yarrow, can be used. Even city-dwellers have many possibilities of collecting decorative plants all year long. Depending on the season, you can collect a variety of flowers, grasses, fruits or seed pods.

Drying

There are different ways to preserve flowers, grasses, fruits or seed pods. To air-dry plants, tie them into bunches and hang them upside down in a dark airy place.

Tip: When you tie plants into a bunch you should use a rubber band since it will tighten as the stems dry and contract.

Instead of air-drying your collected "treasures" for several weeks, you can dry them much more quickly in the oven. Grasses and broad leaves can be placed singly in a row on a baking sheet. Flowers can be inserted, stem first, into a cooling rack or chicken wire so that the heads rest on the wire mesh and the stems hang down vertically.

Important: When you are collecting wild plants you should be extremely careful *not to cut protected, endangered, or poisonous plants!*

People with gardens can plant straw-flowers, certain grasses, baby's breath, etc. to harvest and use for decorative purposes.

Many flowers can be dried, pressed, dyed, or even spray-painted.

Tip: Brown plants can be worked right into the model. Light or colored plants suffer in the heat of the oven. Therefore it is better to attach them to the model after the baking process.

Some of the plants which are nice decorations for saltdough objects.

yarrow

wild hollyhock

geum

poppy

wormwood

butter-and-eggs

grape hyacinth

shepherd's purse

knapweed

Canada thistle

You can dry flowers in about 30 to 40 minutes at low temperature (140° F) depending on how delicate they are.

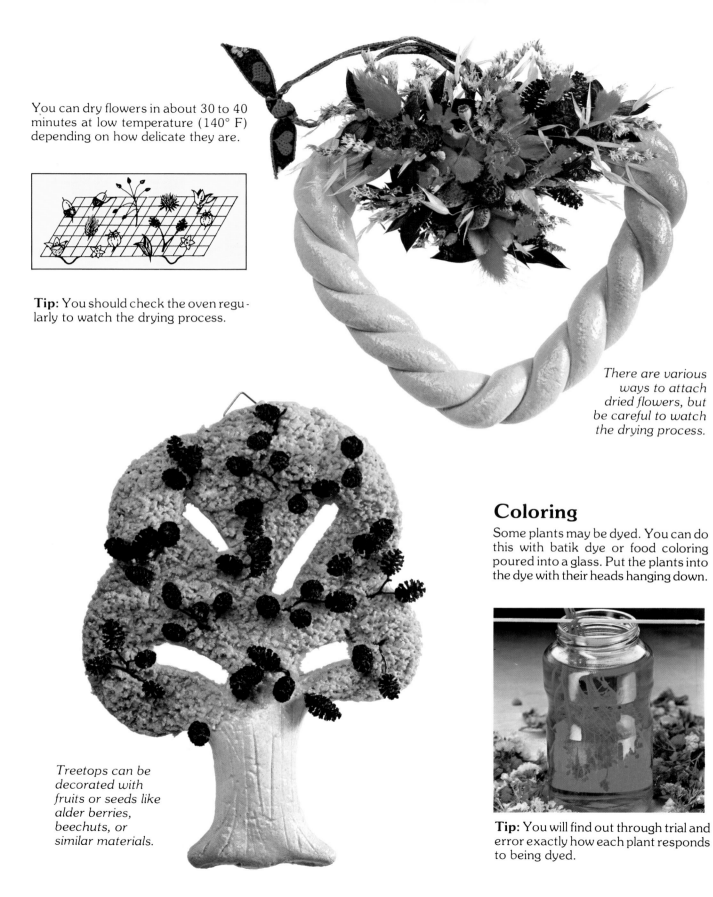

Tip: You should check the oven regularly to watch the drying process.

There are various ways to attach dried flowers, but be careful to watch the drying process.

Coloring

Some plants may be dyed. You can do this with batik dye or food coloring poured into a glass. Put the plants into the dye with their heads hanging down.

Tip: You will find out through trial and error exactly how each plant responds to being dyed.

Treetops can be decorated with fruits or seeds like alder berries, beechuts, or similar materials.

You have to watch, however, that the heads don't sit on the bottom of the glass. They should swim in the liquid. After a few days the plants can be removed from the dye. Carefully blot them with paper towels and then hang them, head down, in a dark airy place to dry completely.

Tip: If you own a convection oven you can speed up the drying process. At 140° F the drying takes about 20 minutes. This is especially ideal for grasses, which become light and fluffy.

Hang up grasses, poppy pods, etc. in full sunlight in order to bleach them.

Natural colors can be deepened with like-colored spray paint, or you may want to spray plants a completely different color, such as gold. When spraying plants, it is advisable to use a shoe box or any other small carton as a shield to contain the excess spray paint.

Attaching

The prepared plants can now be attached to the saltdough models with a hot glue gun or a clear-drying glue.

Depending on the model, you may first want to assemble plants into flower arrangements. These can be bound together with wire or string, then glued in place. A decorative ribbon can hide the juncture.

Varnishing

Spraying the plants with hairspray will accentuate their colors. Repeat this procedure after a while to refresh the colors. Spray varnishes can also be used for a more permanent effect.

Dusting

Dusty arrangements can be cleaned with a hair dryer. Put the hair dryer on its coolest setting and approach the flower arrangement slowly and carefully so that the delicate grasses are not broken by the stream of air.

Working with Natural Materials

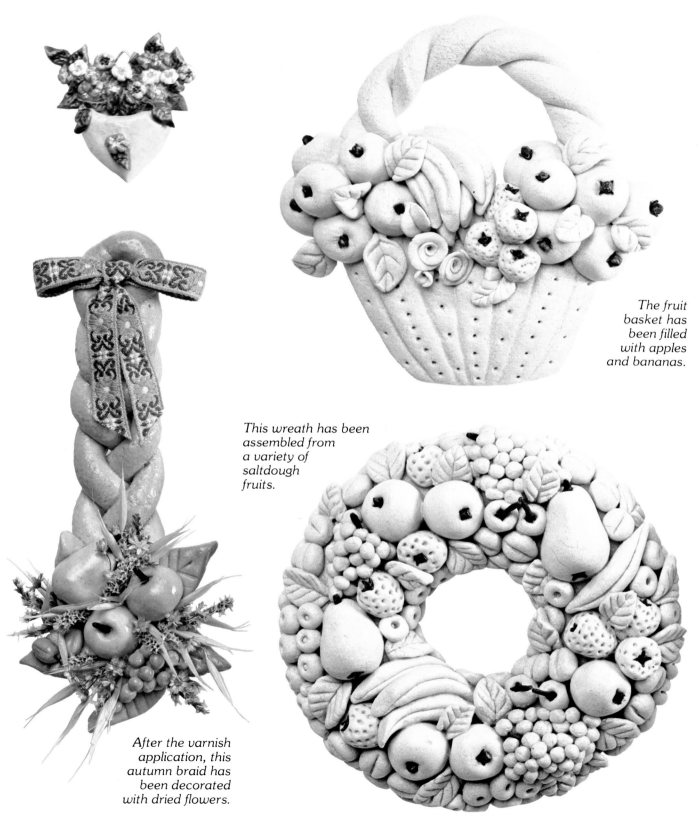

The fruit basket has been filled with apples and bananas.

This wreath has been assembled from a variety of saltdough fruits.

After the varnish application, this autumn braid has been decorated with dried flowers.

Note the modelled loop on this miniature autumn braid. It consists of two dough ropes which are connected. The third dough rope has been cut off.

Moss and Seeds as Leaves, Flowers and Fruit

To make this lush tree, begin by modelling a thin tree top, to which the moss will be added later. Form the tree trunk at the same time as the top. It is best to use colored dough to eliminate the need for painting later. Scratch lines into the trunk with a modellig tool to create the bark effect. Instead of moss, you can also use dried flowers, such as yarrow blossoms.

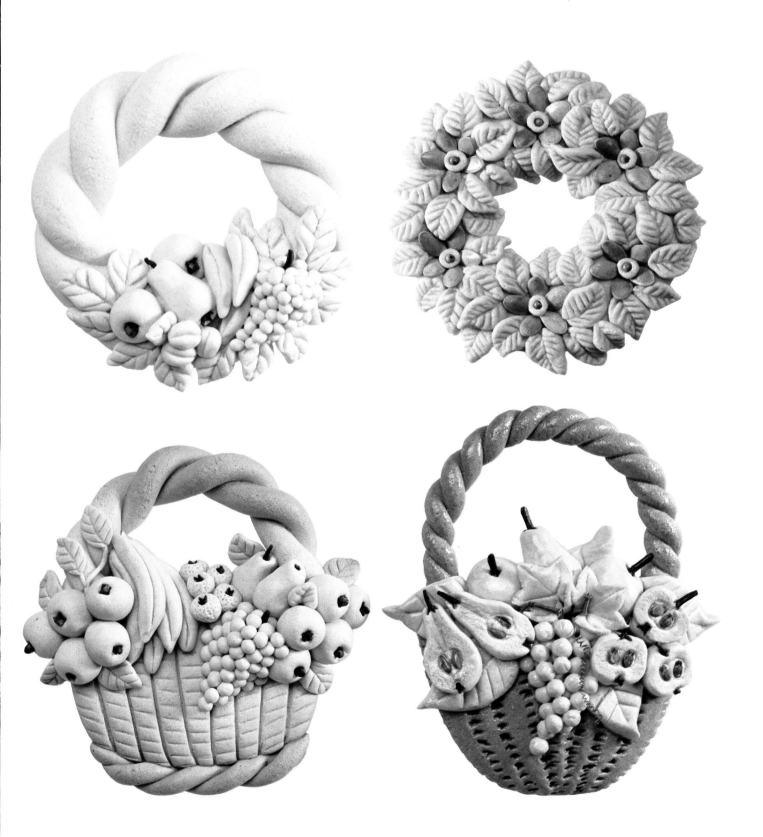

61

MODELLING IDEAS

Cut-Out Forms

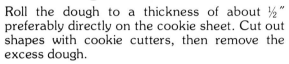

Tip: If the ingredients only say "dough," use the basic recipe:

> 2 cups flour
> 1 cup salt
> ¾ cup water

Variations

Put cut-outs of different sizes on top of each other by moistening the underside of the smaller part with a wet brush and attaching it.

Patterns can be made with many items such as cloves, peppercorns, mustard seeds, cake decorating tips, and button stamps (see "Working with Tools").

Dried flowers can also be added at this time. If this is done, the baking temperature of 250° F should not be exceeded, otherwise the colors will not remain true.

Modelling

Roll the dough to a thickness of about ½" preferably directly on the cookie sheet. Cut out shapes with cookie cutters, then remove the excess dough.

Decorations can now be pressed in with a toothpick, a straw, etc.

Punch a hole with a straw for the hanger. Leave the straw in place to keep the hole open, then remove it after baking approximately one hour.

Small ornaments can be cut out with cookie cutters. They can be decorated with additional dough, spices and glitter.

Tip: Brush the edges of a cut-out ornament well with a wet brush. This makes it easier to smooth out later with a modelling tool. Depending on the model, the string for the hanger can be worked right in.

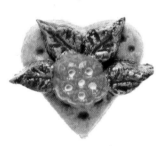

Wreaths and Hearts

For small wreaths or hearts, about 2½″ in diameter, you need about 50g of dough.

Roll the dough ropes to a length of 7″ and twist them into a wreath.

Create a heart by indenting at the seam.

To shape a heart from a twisted wreath, press the wreath at the seam inward and shape the indentation for the heart with index finger and thumb.

Decorations with dough or with dried flowers can be added immediately, or after the baking process.

Important: When you are incorporating dried flowers before the baking, do not allow the temperature to rise above 250° F because the colors will fade.

Fantasy Bird

Size: 6″ x 6½″

Roll the dough about ½″ thick and cut out using a pattern. Smooth the edges with a wet brush. Mark the eye with a berry.

Attach the first row of the tail with dough balls roughly the size of cherries. With a straw or modelling stick, punch holes into them. Next you can add small pea-size balls to the spaces between the bigger ones and, again, press small holes in with a straw.

A second layer of balls and flower designs are attached to the body. You can vary the decoration by using kernels and seeds, always moistening their surfaces first.

Tip: When you are modelling the tail you should be especially careful to keep the parts sufficiently moist or the small dough balls will not adhere.

Heart with Apple

Size: 6″ x 5½″

Roll the dough and cut out using a pattern. Save the remaining dough for the leaves and apple. Brush the edges with a wet brush and smooth them with a modelling tool.

Mark the center of the heart, making a small indentation with your finger, and arrange three leaves around this center. Add the apple in the form of a small ball. The apple is shaped by pressing two cloves into the ball. Press one clove in the top with the little stem sticking out, then press the stem into the bottom so only the bud is visible.

Decorate the heart by pressing a star-shaped decorating tip into the dough. Use a pattern to help shape the birds. Give them each a pepper-corn eye, and create a design with peppercorns on the center of their bodies.

Wreath of Crete

Size: 4″ in diameter

Roll part of the dough ⅛″ thick and cut out with a round cutter that is 2½″ in diameter. This serves as the base onto which you "build" the rest.

Next shape dough slices, ¾″ in diameter, and press a comb onto them. You will need about 11 of these disks for the outer edge of the wreath.

For further decoration, you can alternate rolled-up disks or slices with horizontal or vertical lines pressed into them. To change the pattern you can also form leaves, but for this type of wreath you should bring out the contours, once again with a comb, instead of a modelling tool.

Variations

These wreaths make lovely candle holders which can be varied with the application of leaves, little balls, or small loops. Dough slices and leaves, textured with a comb, can also be added to a braided wreath, and then decorated with modelled birds.

Wreath with Fruit

Size: 8″ in diameter

Make a wreath using two dough rolls of 250g each, forming them into two dough strands, each 24″ long (see page 24, "Twisting Wreaths").

Divide the surface of the wreath into three segments and mark each with a toothpick. Then shape five leaves for each of the three arrangements and attach them to the wreath where shown below.

Next form the pears and arrange them as shown in the illustration. Shape the apples from dough balls 1″ thick, and use a clove for stems and buds. The grapes can be made from small dough balls placed next to each other and on top of each other. Again, wet them with a brush from time to time so that they adhere. The empty places can be filled with plums.

Variations

The fruit wreath can also be decorated with more small dough balls placed on the grooves of the twisted wreath.

You can create a pleasing contrast by using cocoa saltdough for the twisted wreath, and modelling the arrangements, leaves and fruit, from wheat saltdough.

Bread Wreath

You can shape the rolls, pretzels, and bread loaves at the same time, but bake them separately on the baking sheet and not directly on the dough leaves. Glue them on afterwards with a strong glue.

Variation

Make the dough wreath with brown colored dough and the leaves, etc., with white dough. Brush the pretzels shortly before the end of the baking time with corn syrup.

Wreath with Grain

Form a wreath 6½″ in diameter using 300g of dough rolled into two dough ropes, each 19″ long.

After the wreath has been baked and varnished, tie a 20″ long ribbon into a bow around it and glue it in place.

The basic decoration consists of wheat, barley and oats, which are glued onto the wreath (give them extra support if necessary). You can add fine grasses, dried flowers, etc., to the arrangement. Finally you may glue small rolls and pretzels, perhaps strewn with poppy and sesame seeds, on the arrangement.

Wreath
with Oats

As a base for the wreath with oats, prepare a frame out of thin wire. You can attach the stems of the oats closely together on the frame, for fullness. Then, glue small pretzels, rolls, and saltdough braids on the oats.

Variation

A wreath like this can also be made with other kinds of grains. Grasses, combined with dried flowers for a color contrast, also work well.

Small Basket

Size: 5½″ x 6″

Shape 120g of dough into the body of the basket. Roll 50g of dough into two dough ropes, each 6¾″ long. Twist and press them to form the handle on the moistened basket.

For the apples, form a ¾″ thick roll of dough, cut off five slices (each ¾″ thick) and roll them into balls. Press cloves into them, either as stems or buds. For the leaves, cut five

slices (each ½″ thick) and shape them into leaves. Press lines into the basket dough with a ruler. Create the basket weave by putting two forks into the grooves and pressing the dough together. Make two roses and place them on the leaves. Cluster small dough balls together to form a bunch of grapes.

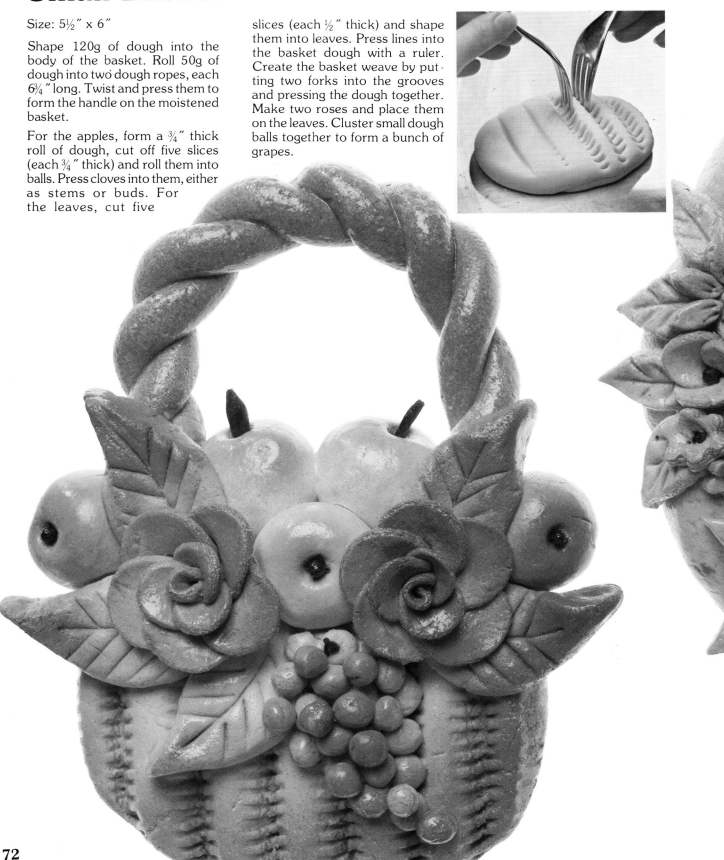

72

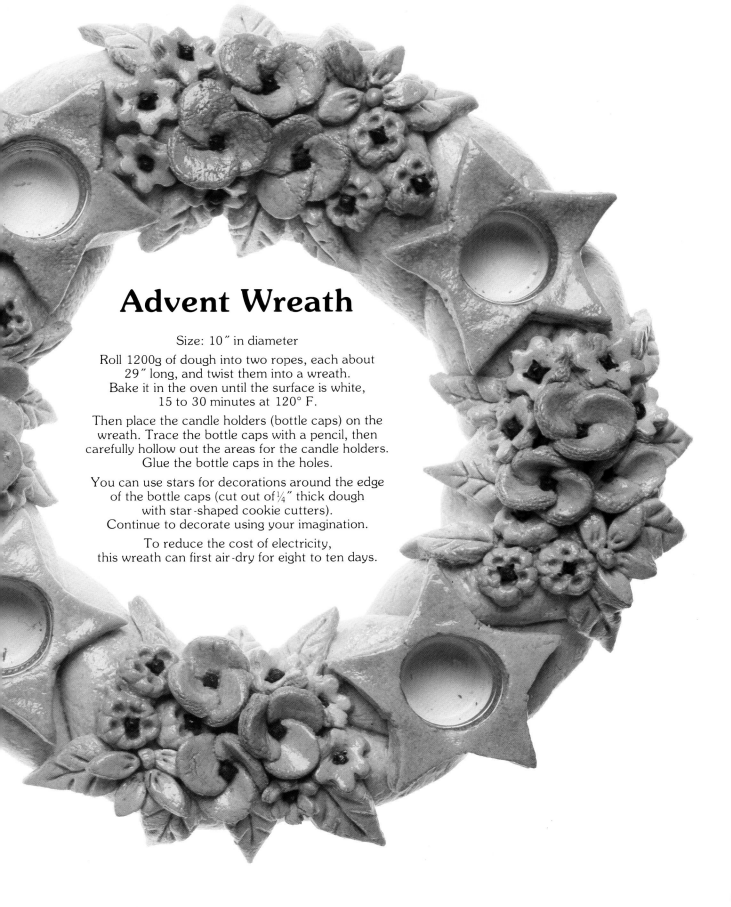

Advent Wreath

Size: 10″ in diameter

Roll 1200g of dough into two ropes, each about
29″ long, and twist them into a wreath.
Bake it in the oven until the surface is white,
15 to 30 minutes at 120° F.

Then place the candle holders (bottle caps) on the
wreath. Trace the bottle caps with a pencil, then
carefully hollow out the areas for the candle holders.
Glue the bottle caps in the holes.

You can use stars for decorations around the edge
of the bottle caps (cut out of ¼″ thick dough
with star-shaped cookie cutters).
Continue to decorate using your imagination.

To reduce the cost of electricity,
this wreath can first air-dry for eight to ten days.

Christmas Decorations

Many different kitchen utensils can be used to model or cut out Christmas tree ornaments, candleholders, and medallions. Small cake tins are often ideal. You can create beautiful designs with a wooden skewer or a marzipan tool.

The angel sitting on a cloud has to be formed in several steps. First, shape the cloud and put the angel's head on it. Once this base is dry you can work upwards. The body and head are modelled around a support cone.

The star made out of straw
may be decorated with tiny
straw flowers and a salt-
dough star in the center.

This Santa comes with a sack full of
toys. It might be fun to make this big
Santa Claus with your children.

The cut-out Christmas tree appears
especially beautiful because of the use of
glitter! Glitter can also be purchased
premixed with liquid glue.

Decorations for windows and Christmas trees, small and large candle holders, gift tags or nice presents for the holidays—all can be created with saltdough.

You can model small Christmas themes from cookie cutters, or you can create stars or ice crystals with thin dough strands.

Painting the edges with gold or silver lends a festive splendor to Christmas ornaments.

Candle holders are easy to shape. Just press the candle into the soft dough to create the desired indentation.

Easter Decorations

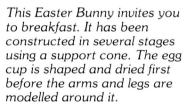

The Easter nests above and below are formed from balls of dough which have had eggs pressed into them. The grass can be made with rough-textured or strainer-pressed dough.

Molds can be bought in hobby shops to make the small pendants pictured across the top.

This Easter Bunny invites you to breakfast. It has been constructed in several stages using a support cone. The egg cup is shaped and dried first before the arms and legs are modelled around it.

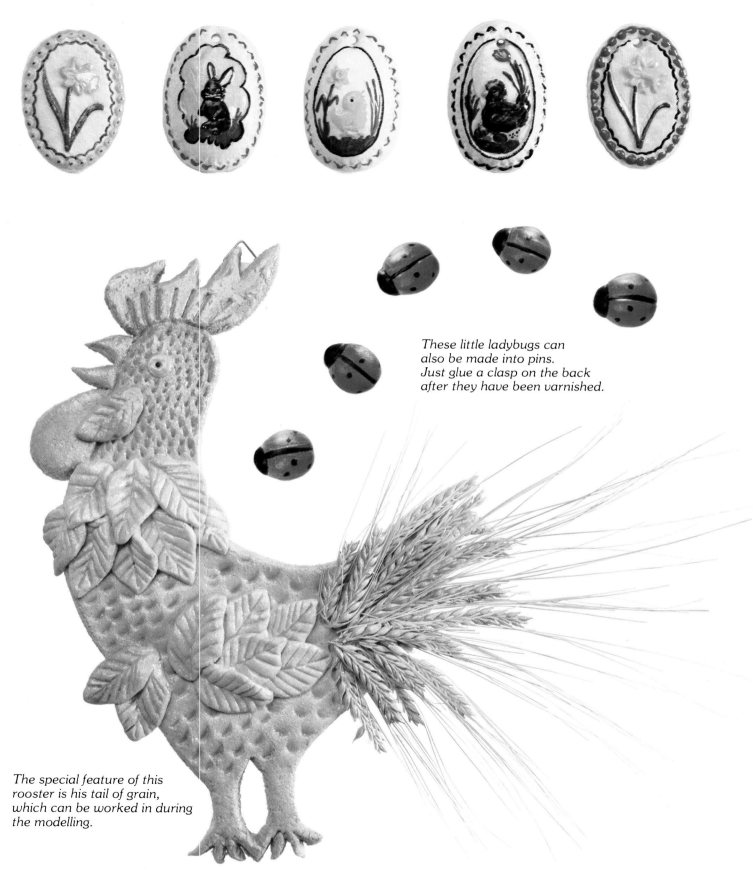

These little ladybugs can
also be made into pins.
Just glue a clasp on the back
after they have been varnished.

The special feature of this
rooster is his tail of grain,
which can be worked in during
the modelling.

Easter Bunnies

Size: 4¾" high

Knead the dough for the body and shape it into a ball, slightly flattening it between the palms of your hands. Use the same principle for the head, the arms and the feet. A carrot can be shaped from a marble-sized piece of dough.

Moisten the connecting points with a brush and put all parts together. Shape the ears about 1¾" long and attach them to the head. Make a hole for a hanger at the top of the head. Insert a piece of a straw and leave it in place for the first two hours of baking, then remove it.

Greek Easter Nest

Size: 4″ x 6″

Roll 220g of dough into a 28″ long rope and twist it as illustrated.

In keeping with Greek tradition, you would place a red Easter egg in the center.

Festive Objects

With simple methods you can create dramatic effects. We used rolled saltdough for this window frame.

Curt + Susanne

Small pendants can be decorated with dried flowers which have been spray-painted gold. The gold should only be applied after the varnishing, or it will oxidize.

The thin pendulum of this clock needs to be reinforced. Roll the dough around a toothpick or a thick piece of wire.

Baby Shower Gifts

A picture of a stork. Baby's personal data can be included to make a very special gift.

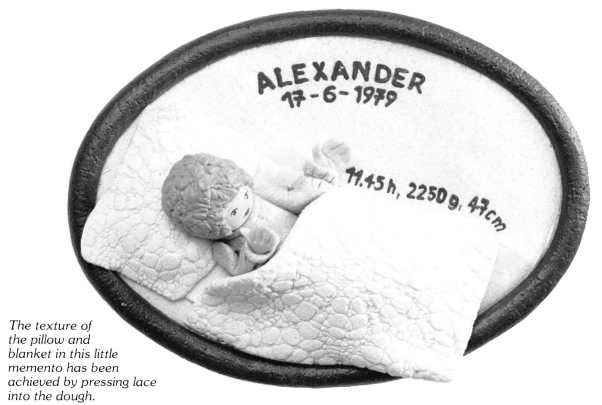

ALEXANDER
17 - 6 - 1979

11.45 h, 2250 g, 47 cm

The texture of the pillow and blanket in this little memento has been achieved by pressing lace into the dough.

This plaque of a child's tiny handprint will be a favorite keepsake.

Apple

Size: 2½″ x 1¾″

Knead the dough and shape it into a ball. Make an indentation in the top and bottom with your thumb. Make a small roll of dough and put it in the upper indentation for a stem. Brush the indentation first with a wet brush. Roll a small ball (½″ in diameter), shape it into a leaf, and attach it at the stem. A small hole can be made with a toothpick at this juncture if the apple is to be hung.

Variation

Instead of painting the apple, brush it before the end of the baking time (at 300° F) with a mixture of milk and water. Then turn the oven temperature up to 400° F, if desired, and watch the browning process closely.

Mouse

Size: 2½″ x 1¾″

Roll 50g of dough into a ball. Pinch one end with thumb and index finger into a nose. Mark the eyes and the nose with a toothpick.

Form the ears from 2 marble-sized balls. Press 2 slits for the ears into the head, moisten them with a brush and put an ear into each slit.

Punch a hole for the tail. Dip the end of a string in water, then push the wet end into the hole with a toothpick.

Small Hearts

Size: 2½″ x 2½″

Knead the dough well and roll into a ball. Make an indentation in the upper part with your thumb. Make a tip by pressing the dough between thumb and index finger.

It is very easy to model small figurines. As good-luck charms or as small remembrances, they can make charming gifts.

Bird

Roll 100g of dough into a small ball and shape it into a bird. The dough should be dry and elastic.

Slow drying is essential to prevent cracking. The best result is achieved by using the combined drying technique of air and oven.

Clear varnish makes this
saltdough Advent wreath
durable for many years.

In the Rustic Tradition

The natural color of these saltdough figures and basket accentuates the character of rustic and country-style furniture.

The full, rounded forms of these decorations bring out
the warm colors of the dough extremely well, creating a
special cozy feeling.

Saltdough for Children

Circus

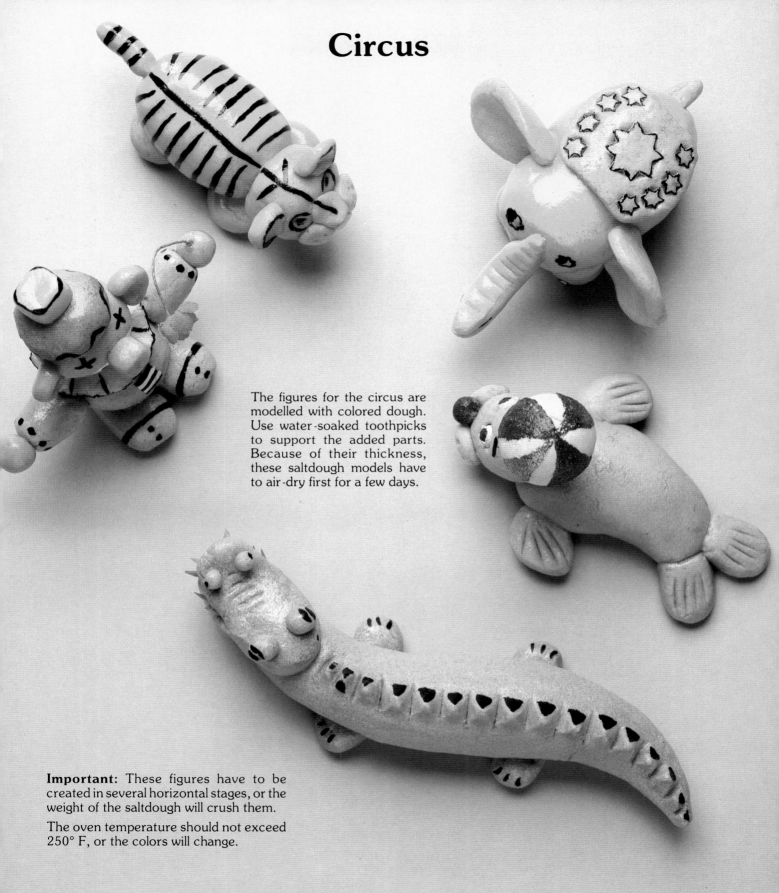

The figures for the circus are modelled with colored dough. Use water-soaked toothpicks to support the added parts. Because of their thickness, these saltdough models have to air-dry first for a few days.

Important: These figures have to be created in several horizontal stages, or the weight of the saltdough will crush them.

The oven temperature should not *exceed* 250° F, or the colors will change.

A Saltdough Zoo

For the plaque shown right, begin by making a saltdough base and baking it. After it is cool, you can start forming the picture. Build a framework for the roof. Put down a strip of dough for each row of shingles on which you place the pre-dried shingles. Start at the lowest row and work upward. Shape the tomcat from brown dough, or paint it with watercolor. For technical reasons, the "tied knot" is only simulated.

Use regular unpainted dough for the pig. Push the nostrils in with a bamboo skewer or a chopstick.

The basket for this cat family has been made from colored dough. Mother cat and her kittens are painted with watercolors.

Use wheat dough, or dough which has been colored with coffee, for this elephant. Most of the parts are shaped from rolls of dough. The wire loop has been pushed into the dough before baking.

The little squirrel has been given a lush brown-colored tail. The nut and the paws are also accentuated with brown colored dough.

Use rolled saltdough to form the window. The owls are partially shaped from colored dough. The arched window turns brown during the baking process.

This charming little koala bear's body is made from two thick dough balls.

Owls

These models are for people who love owls. The examples illustrate some of the variations of owl designs.

During the modelling, a twig of a beech tree has been pressed into the lower part of the body. The claws are then placed over it.

In order to avoid disturbing the delicate feathers, you should touch the owls only on the sides of the head. The color contrast is achieved by dyeing the dough differently.

Making Dolls

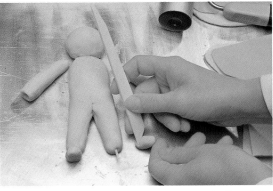

When modelling dolls it is easiest to start with a cone shaped body. Cut the lower part in the center for the legs. Insert water-soaked tooth-picks to join body and head, and half a toothpick at each connection of legs and feet for strength.

The arms should be thicker toward the hands. Depending on the model, they can be attached now or later when the clothing is added.

The feet are shaped from two dough balls of the same size. Lightly indent the top third of the ball with a modelling tool, bend the front part of the foot slightly upward, and then push the back part onto the toothpick.

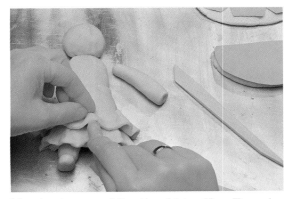

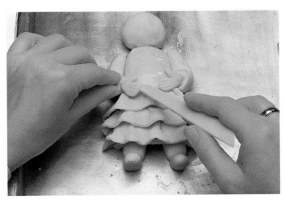

Now begin assembling the skirt ruffles. To make the skirt appear fuller, place a petticoat over the legs and arrange the ruffles over it, starting with the lowest row and working up.

Next the arms can be attached to the body. With a modelling tool press two notches into the arms at the elbows so that the arms bend more easily.

Shape the hands from small balls resembling mittens. With a modelling stick press a small hole in the lower part of the arm and push the hand in. Carefully secure the hand with the modelling tool.

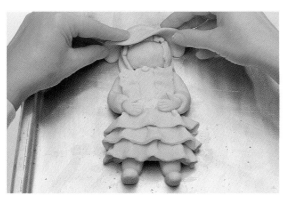

Place two ruffles over the shoulders down to the waist. The hair can be cut out following the pattern. It can then be textured with a small kitchen knife.

Doll Clothing

As soon as the basic shape of the doll has been finished, it is best to cut paper patterns for the clothes. Take a piece of paper and place it over the doll. This will give you a rough idea of the size needed. It is important to cut the paper wide enough for the neckline and the armholes.

Now place the pattern on thinly rolled dough and cut it out. The dough for the clothing should not be too soft for ruffles and pleats. If necessary, the folds can be supported with decorating tips until they are slightly dry and keep their shape.

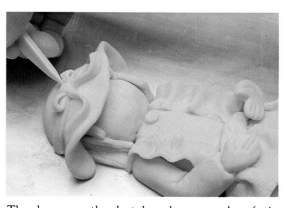

Use the pattern for the hat but leave the dough in the back a little thicker.

The bow on the hat has been made of six individual parts.

Place a small thin ribbon across the hat. In the center, place one loop of the bow to the left and one to the right. Repeat this with two ribbons which are lying on their sides, cutting the ends diagonally. Position the knot over these parts.

Figures on Medallions, or with Cloth

A little doll's fashion show demonstrates how clothing can vary. You don't always have to clothe the figures with saltdough dresses. Small scraps of cloth are often enough to put together skirts, blouses, pants, etc. The figures are dressed after they have been painted.

The cook gets a lacy apron and a scarf around her head with a knot on the forehead.

This figure's blue dress has been cut out of cloth and then glued on. The skirt has been arranged into folds. A velvet ribbon serves as a belt.

The dough base for this medallion is cut out of thinly rolled dough. You may use cookie cutters, a glass or a cup.

The scooter is only indicated with thin dough ribbons.

Each piece of clothing for this reading boy has been modelled separately and then put on the pre-modelled figure.

White lace accentuates this dark blue velvet dress nicely and gives the little doll a festive air. White painted stockings further adorn her Sunday outfit.

Real denim and a striped sweater add a special flair to this boy. Two hearts—as red as the cheeks— serve as pants pockets.

Figures from Fairy-Tales

The imagination of children is particularly stimulated by themes from fairy-tales. They can express themselves creatively while modelling with saltdough.

With saltdough you can create beautiful scenes from fairy-tales just like this picture of a windmill. For this picture, the windmill has been formed first and the miller later. Finally, two rectangles have been formed with a pointed knife to resemble a wheatfield.

For the picture with the gnome, you start with the mushroom house, then add the door with doorhandle, letterbox, ladybug and chimney. Then form the gnome. The yard is created on a roll of dough which is put under the house and decorated with flowers. All the little details are added afterward.

The colors on these two figures are thickly applied and cover well.

The mouth is just a curved line with the corners of the mouth marked.

Themes from fairy tales and the world of animals offer an inexhaustible supply of ideas. As wall plaques, they present an imaginative alternative to posters and photos.

A Parade of Figures

An outing with children holding a pinwheel, a teddy bear and a little doll is beautifully captured on a wooden board. Each figure has been modelled separately, then dried and painted. The treetop has also been glued on to the tree after the drying process. Finally, the little bird has been added to the tree.

For the grandmother's knitting needles, you can use toothpicks, which can be baked in.

These two grave looking gentlemen—one a dentist, the other a lawyer—are easily modelled from saltdough.

Painted wall plaques
make very nice hostess
gifts, especially when the
theme reflects the oc -
casion for the invitation.

Stout Farmers

A decorative farm couple in matching colors adds a nice touch to any country style decor. The farmer's wife's braided hairstyle is especially elaborate. Both figures are holding dried flowers.

When you are painting such figures it is important to cover all areas well with a thick coat of paint. This gives the figures an even more solid look. You may still reinforce it by applying several coats of varnish. Each coat has to be completely dry before the next one is applied.

Masks

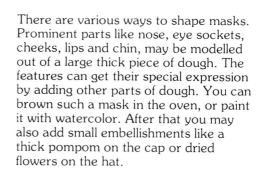

There are various ways to shape masks. Prominent parts like nose, eye sockets, cheeks, lips and chin, may be modelled out of a large thick piece of dough. The features can get their special expression by adding other parts of dough. You can brown such a mask in the oven, or paint it with watercolor. After that you may also add small embellishments like a thick pompom on the cap or dried flowers on the hat.

When you are painting the masks with watercolor you can blend in the color of the cheeks nicely. The transition to the skin color is easily achieved. Choose a brown tone for eyes rather than black. Wrinkles in the face are marked with darker shading.

Tip: The surface of colored dough models should not be brushed with water because these moistened areas would change colors during the drying or baking process. Therefore it is advisable to moisten the underside and press it onto the dry part.

Sun-Catchers

Cut designs out with small cookie cutters. After the drying process, glue colored tissue paper on the back.

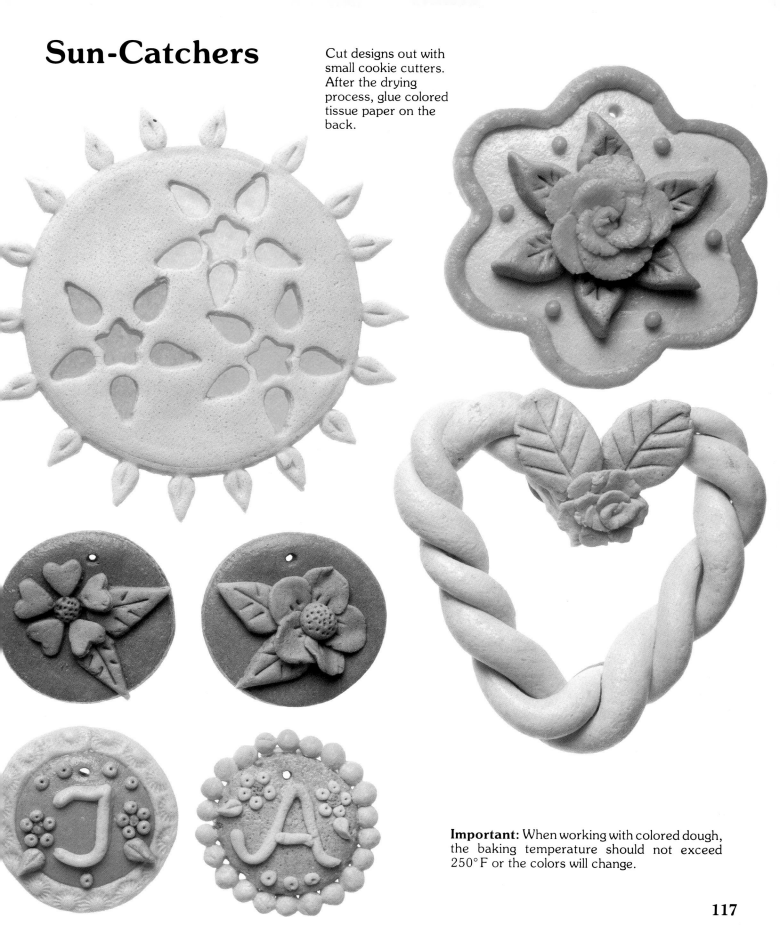

Important: When working with colored dough, the baking temperature should not exceed 250° F or the colors will change.

Single motifs can be arranged into lovely
wall decorations. You can add
one piece at a time.

Heart with Flowers

You can let your imagination run wild while you are making this heart. The blossoms are modelled separately and are then arranged on a heart-shaped ribbon. Roughen the spaces between the blossoms with a modelling tool. Paint the blossoms after they are dried. Ideal colors are various shades of yellow or purple. You may add either red to yellow and get orange, or add white to purple and get lighter shades of purple like the delicate shade of lilac.

Summer Hat

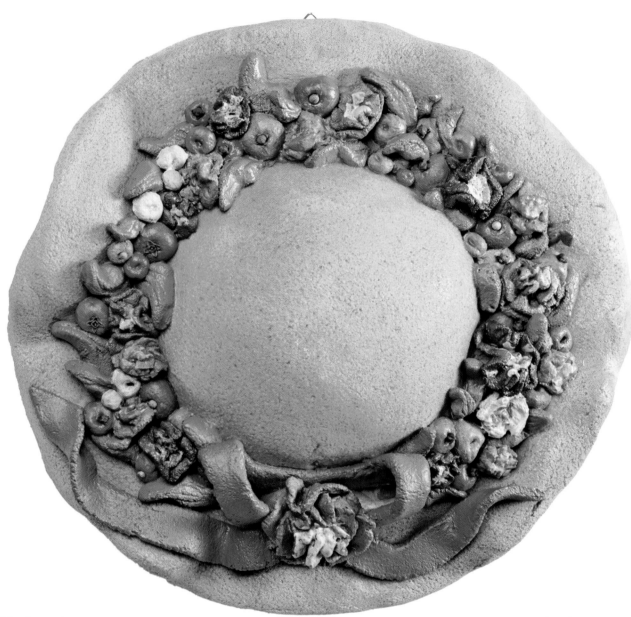

The basic form is
a circle of dough which is
supported in the center by a bowl.
The edges are slightly lifted up before the
drying process to give the hat a look of
elegance. These areas can be given support
by aluminum foil,
decorating tips, or plastic
coated cardboard. The actual
decoration of the hat begins with the
modelling of a flower wreath and the addition
of a bow. After cooling, it can be painted.

Alphabet Tray

In this alphabet, each little saltdough piece has its own special meaning: in each little box is an object whose first initial is the same as the letter from the alphabet.

The background is a thin framed piece of wood. Each box is again framed by thinner strips of wood, or simply by drawn lines. The saltdough pieces have to be very delicate. Therefore this project requires a lot of time and patience.

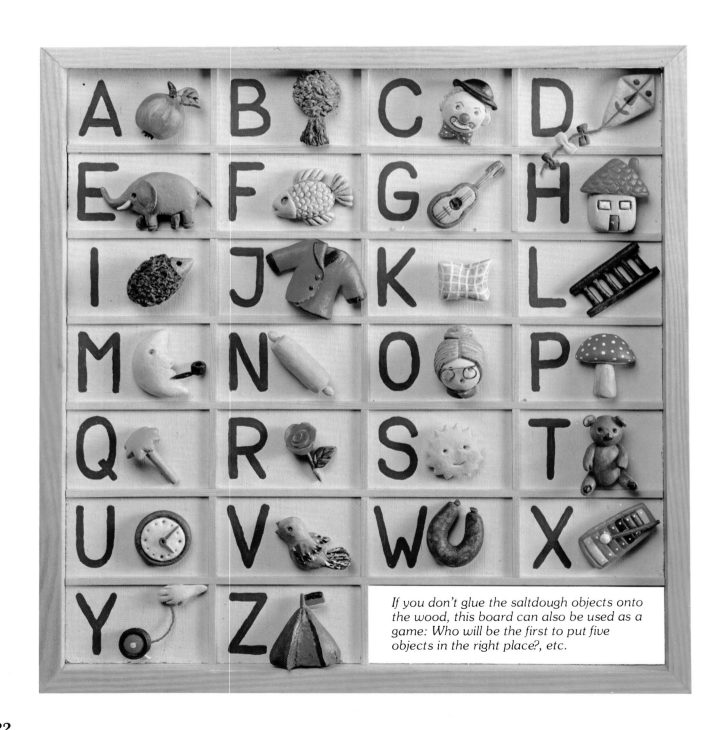

If you don't glue the saltdough objects onto the wood, this board can also be used as a game: Who will be the first to put five objects in the right place?, etc.

Woman with Flowers on a Plaque

It is best to use a wooden board as a base for this picture of a flower woman. For example, you might use a wooden plate. Glue the modelled, painted and varnished figure onto the plate and add dried flowers, moss or other material. Natural tones, as well as shades of green, are best suited for the clothing.

Trees

Shape the tree in one piece. First form the trunk, then flatten the upper part with a rolling pin.

Sheep

Roll the dough ⅛″ thick, then cut out, following the pattern, and smooth the edges with a modelling tool.

Moisten the area that is to be covered with fleece. To make fleece, press dough through a garlic press (filling the garlic press about three times) and distribute it over the sheep, leaving the legs uncovered.

Mark eyes and ears with a toothpick. Shape a small ear and press it into the marked hole. For variation, use brown dough for the body and white dough for the fleece.

Cut the branches out following the pattern.

The treetop can be created either with dough from a garlic press, or with pieces of dough of different thickness roughened with a wooden skewer.

Paint this tree and decorate it with small dried flowers. Press small dough cherries on the textured treetop.

Shepherd's Scene

You can assemble complete pictures and scenes with animals and people, and leave them either natural color or paint them.

Small additional decorations like fences or grass patches further heighten the effect. Framed bulletin boards covered with burlap are the ideal background for such small saltdough pictures.

Saltdough Pictures

You can create beautiful pictures with saltdough. For instance, you may use a ceramic tile as a background or you may paint a landscape on paper and glue a saltdough tree over it. Saltdough tiles are made from a firm dough mixed with wallpaper paste. Whether you model right on the fresh tile or later on the dried one depends on the subject.

A High Relief

The apple tree picture combines relief as well as sculpture techniques. The tree and the girl are modelled as a relief while the boy on the ladder has been formed like a sculpture. The grass area protrudes from the picture.

For the tree trunk and the fork in the branches we used a real wooden branch whose bark had been peeled off. Other natural materials in this picture have been incorporated for the nest, the food in the mother bird's beak, and the little flowers in the meadow. The girl's jump-rope is cotton string.

The nest has been made from grasses which are pressed into the moist saltdough. Cut the saltdough birds beaks with pointed scissors.

Shape the boy as described in the chapter on "Sculptures."

The apple basket is modelled as a sculpture. You get the basket-weave texture by pinching the moist saltdough with tweezers.

Framed Picture of a Gnome

This picture is made according to the size of the frame, but the frame is only added after the drying. The bench is a piece of wood worked into the dough; the gnome is modelled over it.

Once the fence and the sunflowers are made, the mushrooms with the hedgehog may be added. As soon as the picture is totally dry, the tree top is modelled over the frame.

Free Standing Object

Forming the tiled stove and all the many details is a time-consuming but enjoyable project. First make the basic stove. The half circle for the storage area of wood may be cut out with a round cookie cutter. Use slightly rough pieces of dough for the lower part of the stove. Cut in the grooves for the tiles with a knife. The round disks for the tiles are prepared separately and are then attached to the tiles.

The round disks for the tiles are modelled separately and centered between the grooves of the tiles.

The vase has been formed around a wooden skewer and is therefore hollow.

With a lot of patience you may try to knit a miniature scarf with thin toothpicks.

The logs are shaped from saltdough.

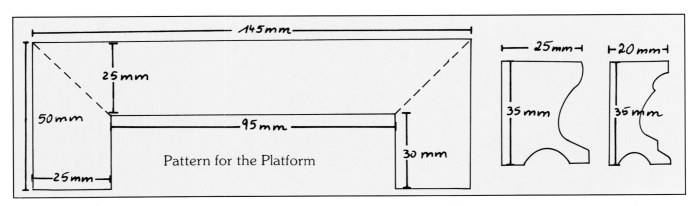

Pattern for the Platform

145mm

25mm

50mm

95mm

25mm

30 mm

25mm

35 mm

20 mm

35 mm

Breadbasket

Sizes of the different parts:

Pretzel: 2½″ x 3″; amount of dough: 40g, rolled to a length of 11″.

Buns: 2″ in diameter; amount of dough: 40g, large star-shaped tip.

Poppy seed roll: 4½″ to 5″ long; amount of dough: 40g, rolled up from a triangle of 5½″ x 2¾″, with the corners a little bit tucked in.

Pretzel

Size: 3¼″ x 4″

Knead the dough thoroughly and roll out to a length of about 17″, leaving the center section slightly thicker.

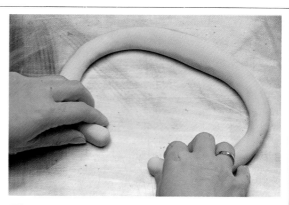

Then form the shape of a pretzel and press the ends on top of it.

With a sharp knife cut a slit into the thicker part.

Variation: During the last hour of baking, brush the pretzel evenly with a mixture of corn syrup and water, leaving the slit unbrushed. You can intensify the browning by raising the temperature.

Important: Since corn syrup is water-absorbent, it is important for the pretzel to be totally dry before varnishing it.

Roll the dough for the base and the cover to a thickness of about 1″ directly on the cookie sheet.

Important: The diameter of the top must be larger than the base since the heart-decorated side piece will be wrapped around the base.

Cut an air hole into the top for the candle. Roll the side strip ("jacket") ½″ thick. The length depends on the diameter or the perimeter of the base. The height should be about 2½″. You can create a design in the dough using small cookie cutters.

Lanterns

Roll the dough out on a cookie sheet ½″ thick.

For the candle holder, you need:

    Two disks each 6″ in diameter

    Seven or eight disks each 2½″ in diameter.

Cut a 2½″ diameter hole into one of the larger disks (air hole for the candle). Cut a ¾″ hole into each small disk.

Scratch the surface with a modelling stick from the center outwards.

Finishing: Connect the small disks with the base and with each other using glue.

Tip: Use these candle holders for their decorative effect when lighted, rather than functionally as warmers.

134

Figurines

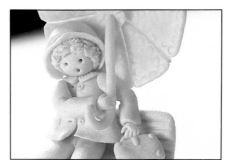

The umbrella's handle must be reinforced with wire or a toothpick.

It has always been mankind's desire to recreate the human body with malleable materials. Creating sculptures from saltdough is a new way of doing so. In order to do it we have developed various techniques as you will discover by studying this night watchman.

The night watchman has been formed in several steps. Begin by modelling the front part and drying it. It is important to give the arm good support. A description of the construction may be found in the chapter "Assembling Sculptures" (page 52). Attach the hat only after the figure has been completely finished and dried. The halberd is a wooden skewer with a saltdough tip.

The backside of the sculpture has been formed just as accurately as the front. The pieces of clothing have been put on separately.

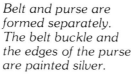

Belt and purse are formed separately. The belt buckle and the edges of the purse are painted silver.

The lantern is made from cardboard and tissue paper. The handle is shaped from wire.

Jewelry

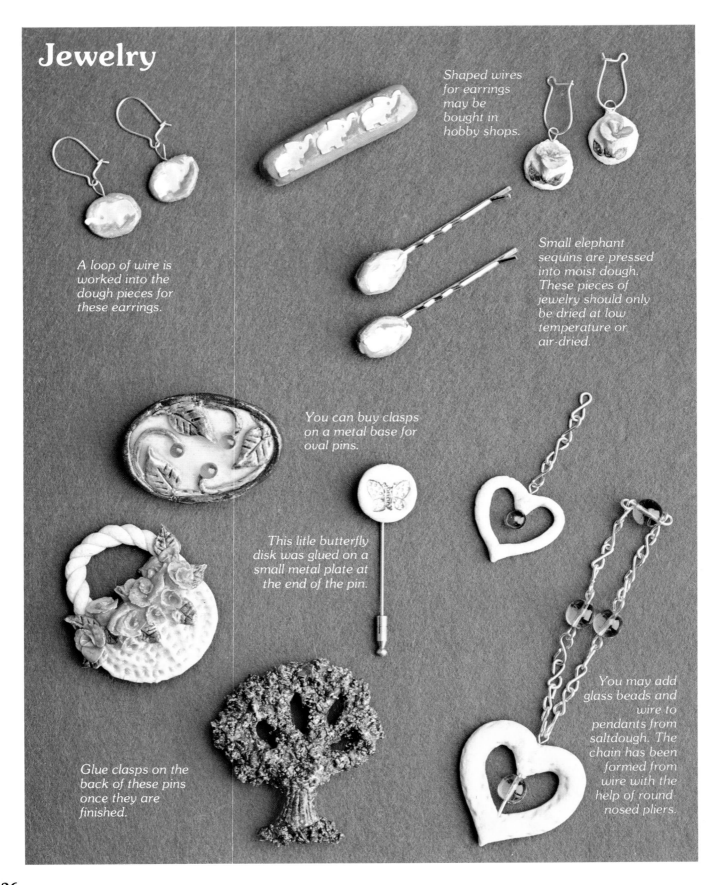

A loop of wire is worked into the dough pieces for these earrings.

Shaped wires for earrings may be bought in hobby shops.

Small elephant sequins are pressed into moist dough. These pieces of jewelry should only be dried at low temperature or air-dried.

You can buy clasps on a metal base for oval pins.

This little butterfly disk was glued on a small metal plate at the end of the pin.

Glue clasps on the back of these pins once they are finished.

You may add glass beads and wire to pendants from saltdough. The chain has been formed from wire with the help of round-nosed pliers.

The saltdough beads are connected into a bracelet with loops made out of silver or brass wire.

Rectangular beads may be worked into a bracelet. Pull a piece of elastic through and knot it.

These pendants are made from marbleized dough. The treated dough has to be rolled thin. Then the pendants are cut out.

Depending on the size of the saltdough beads, it is possible to punch two holes into them.

These flower pins are made from small picture frames with pressed dried flowers glued on. The color of the frame should correspond with the color of the flower.

Patterns

The patterns show the original size of the models.

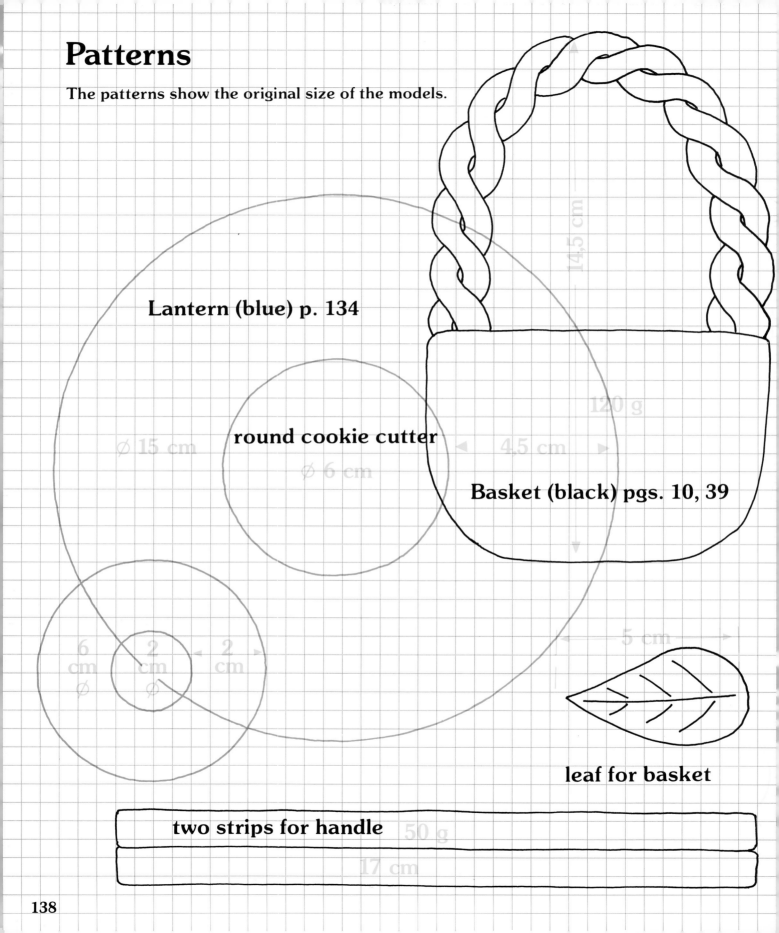

Lantern (blue) p. 134

round cookie cutter

Ø 15 cm

Ø 6 cm

14,5 cm

120 g

4,5 cm

Basket (black) pgs. 10, 39

6 cm Ø

2 cm Ø

2 cm

5 cm

leaf for basket

two strips for handle

50 g

17 cm

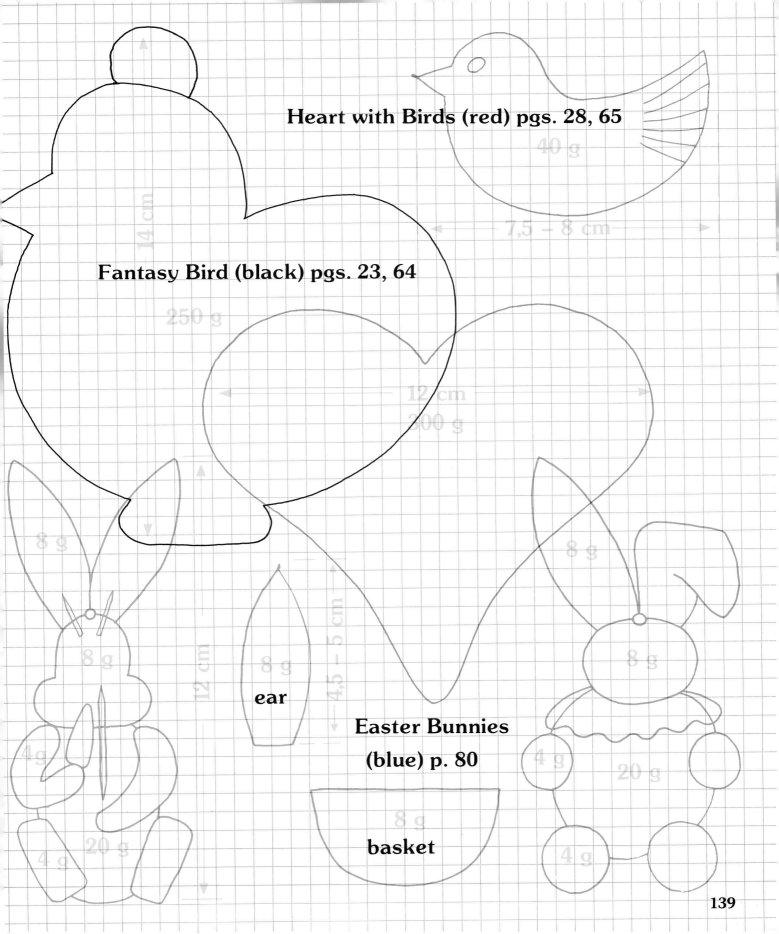

Heart with Birds (red) pgs. 28, 65

40 g

7,5 – 8 cm

Fantasy Bird (black) pgs. 23, 64

14 cm

250 g

12 cm
300 g

8 g

8 g

8 g

8 g

4,5 – 5 cm

12 cm

8 g

ear

Easter Bunnies

(blue) p. 80

4 g

20 g

4 g

basket

4 g

20 g

4 g

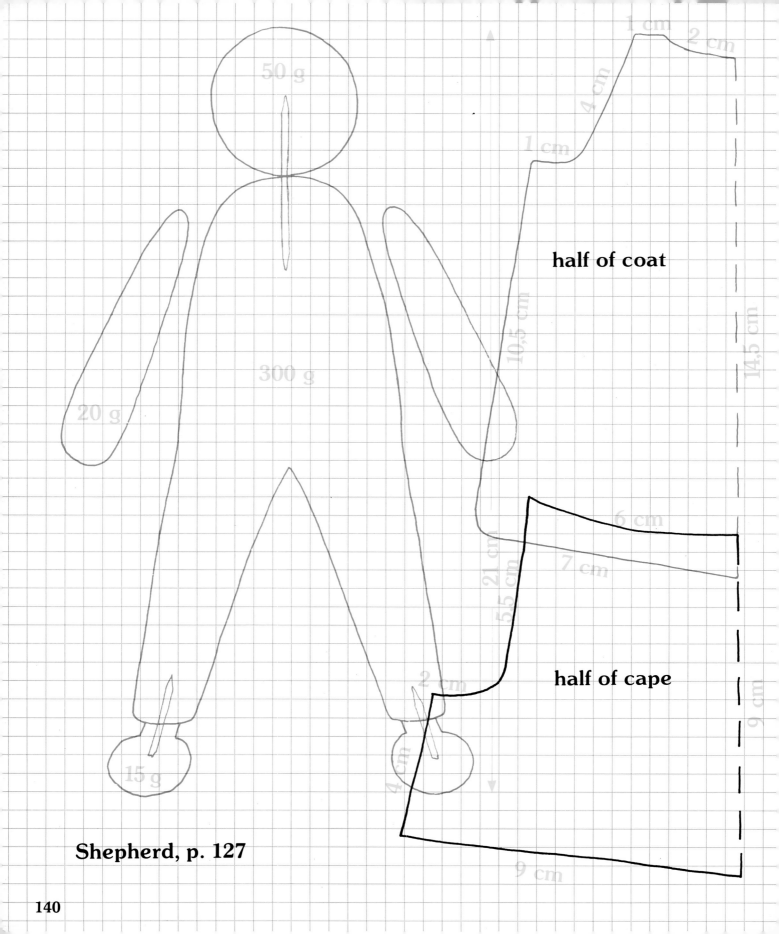

50 g

20 g

300 g

half of coat

1 cm

2 cm

4 cm

1 cm

10,5 cm

14,5 cm

6 cm

7 cm

21 cm

5,5 cm

half of cape

2 cm

4 cm

9 cm

15 g

9 cm

Shepherd, p. 127

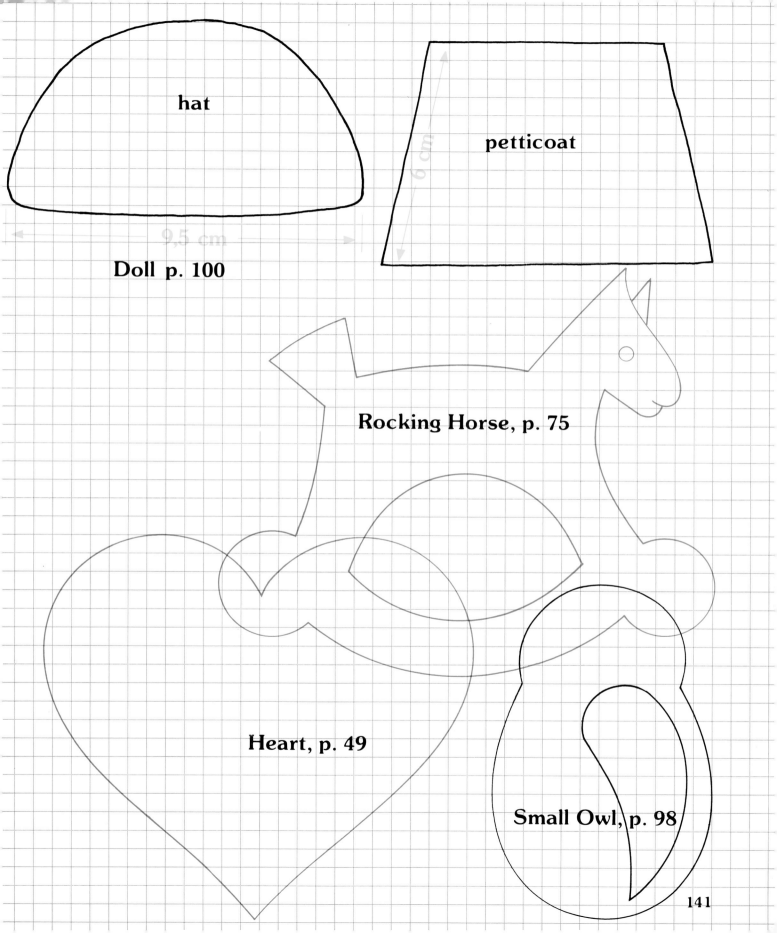

hat

petticoat

6 cm

9,5 cm

Doll p. 100

Rocking Horse, p. 75

Heart, p. 49

Small Owl, p. 98

141

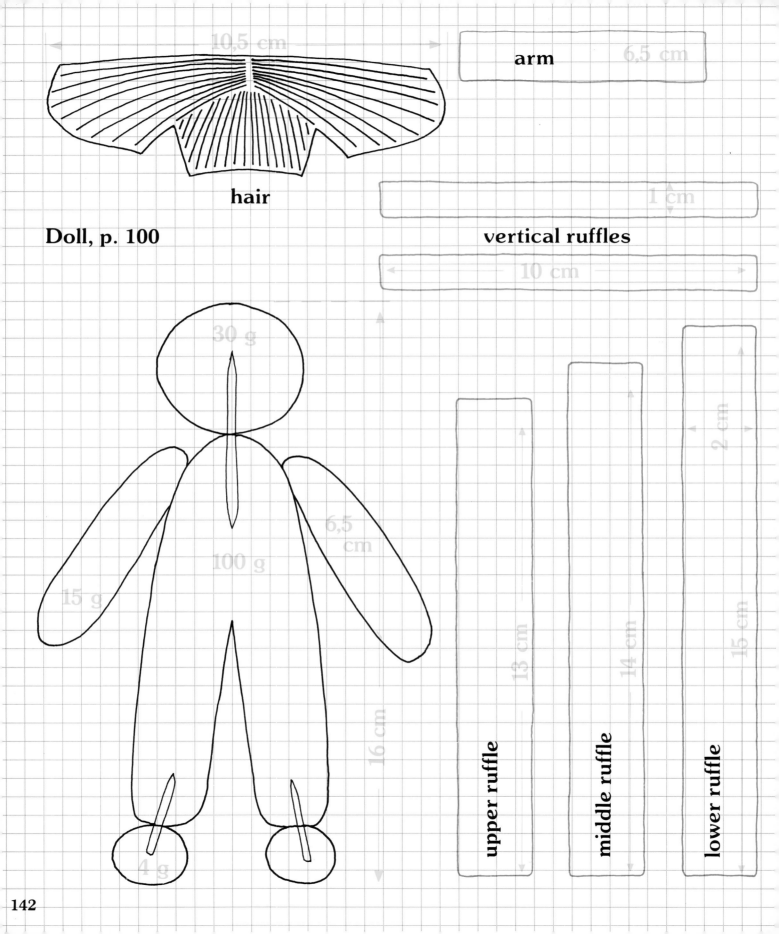

10,5 cm

hair

arm   6,5 cm

Doll, p. 100

1 cm

vertical ruffles

10 cm

30 g

6,5 cm

100 g

15 g

2 cm

16 cm

13 cm

14 cm

15 cm

4 g

upper ruffle

middle ruffle

lower ruffle

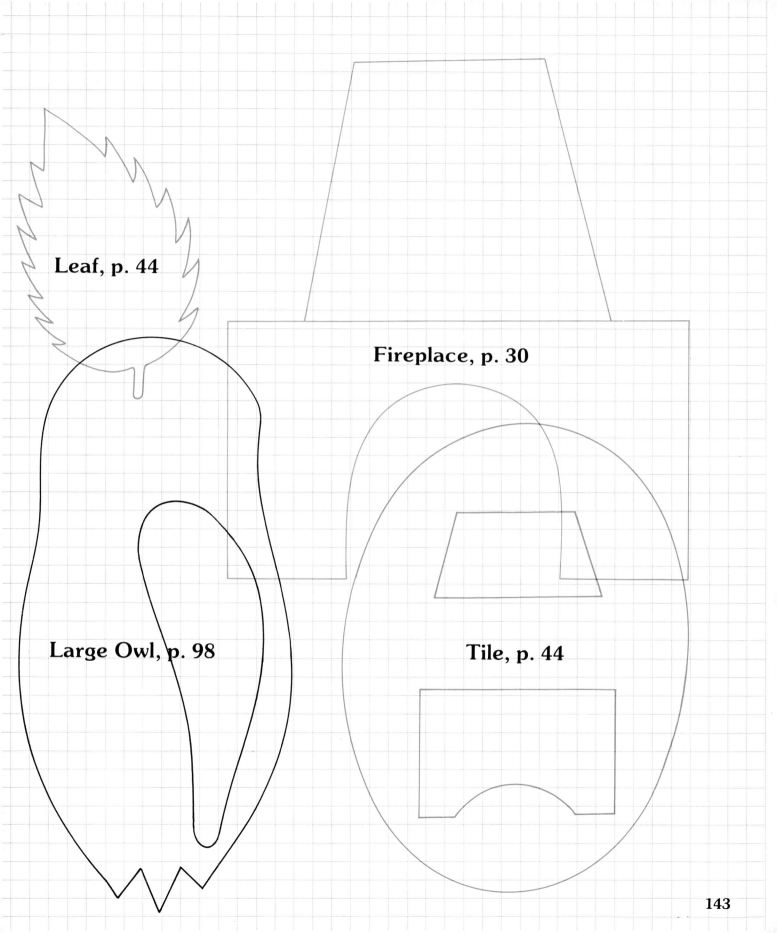

Leaf, p. 44

Fireplace, p. 30

Large Owl, p. 98

Tile, p. 44

143

INDEX